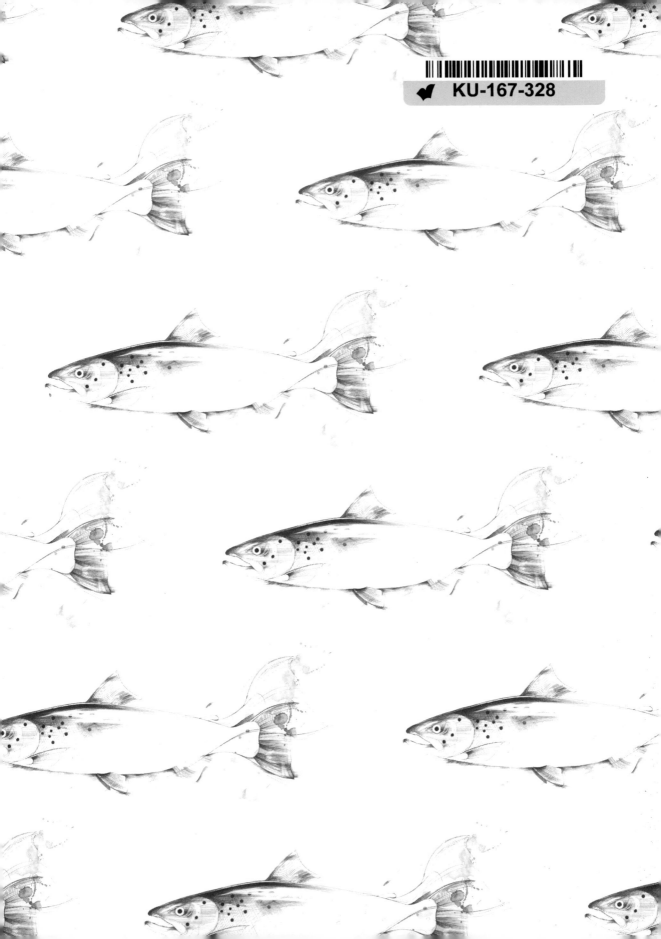

Eric Morecambe
ON FISHING

Eric Morecambe
ON FISHING

Illustrations by David Hughes

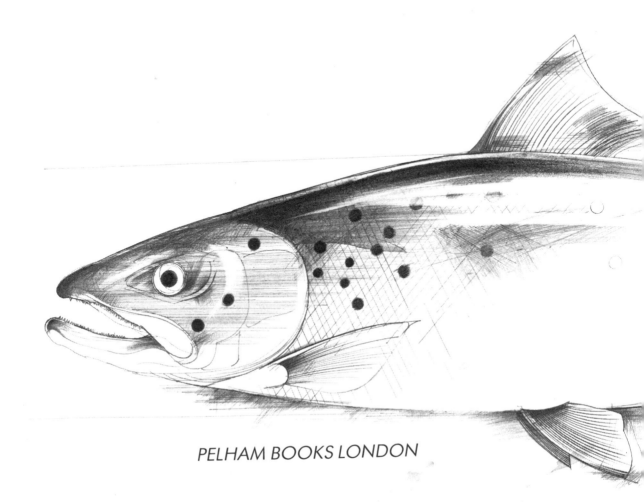

PELHAM BOOKS LONDON

First published in Great Britain by
Pelham Books Ltd
44 Bedford Square, London WC1B 3DU
1984

British Library Cataloguing in Publication Data
Morecambe, Eric
Eric Morecambe on Fishing.
1. Fishing – Anecdotes, facetiae, satire, etc.
I. Title
799.1'2'0207   SH439

ISBN 0 7207 1532 6

Made by Lennard Books
Mackerye End, Harpenden, Herts AL5 5DR

Editor Michael Leitch
Designed by David Pocknell's Company Ltd
Production by Reynolds Clark Associates Ltd
Printed and bound in Yugoslavia by
Mladinska Knjiga, Ljubljana

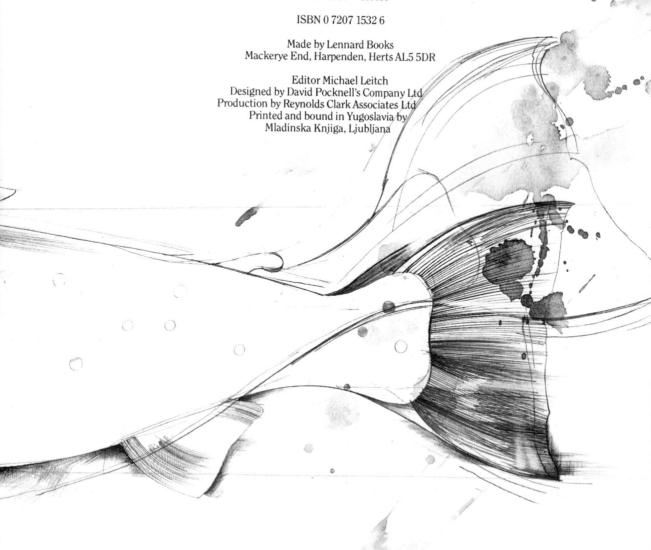

CONTENTS

FOREWORD

The fascination of fishing is completely lost on me. I know I may incense a few fishermen but I am unable to understand the logic of sitting on a river bank, sometimes in pouring rain, fiddling about with flies, lead weights, wet bread, hooks and line or maggots in tins. Eric told me a story once about his dad, who was also a fisherman, sat on the bus. He opened a tin of maggots and they flew into the air having all changed into bluebottles! That must have been a rare moment.

I know Eric used to go fishing with his dad when he was a boy, although my earliest memory was one day in variety going out into the country with a then famous comic called Leon Cortez for a day's trout fishing. All Eric and I did was watch and eat our sandwiches. When we were rehearsing our TV show Eric would often go fishing with our producer Johnny Ammonds on a stretch of the River Kennet. They would be dressed up all day in their fishing hats talking about how to cast and looking at their flies. You can imagine how much rehearsal we got – it was another world of which I was no part.

All I do know is that Eric loved his fishing. I'm sure he enjoyed the peace and quiet and to get away from the hectic life of show business. I would like to think he is doing it right now.

Ernie Wise

THE THREE Fs

This opening chapter is really an Introduction in disguise. A lot of people don't read ordinary Introductions to books any more. I think that is a pity, but there you are. It's a sign of the times. People are in such a hurry. They can't wait to get on to the Big Stuff - the main action, the drama, the taut emotions and the quivering lips, all building up to the saucy bit on page 57 which they heard about at work. So, they skip the Introduction.

To prevent that happening with our book, we have given the Introduction a different kind of title - something with a bit of spice to it, a touch of Eastern promise. That way, no-one will realize it *is* an Introduction, and we'll get all our readers packed in and behaving themselves from the start.

It's exactly the same at Luton Town. If we want a big crowd on a Saturday afternoon, we don't advertise it as a football match. No, what happens is, one of the groundstaff goes outside at two o'clock and hangs up a sign saying 'Strip Show'. The ground is full by ten past, and then we lock the gates until twenty to five.

But we are getting a little bit ahead of our story. The Three Fs, you see, are my hobbies - football, fishing and fotography. And that is possibly the last mention that will be made here of football. My other two hobbies have rather more in common. They are about going out into nature and discovering the art of looking around and enjoying all the things that are happening, particularly amongst the animal life.

Most of the subjects I photograph in nature are birds (and most of the fish I catch are fish). And with each of these hobbies I love to surround myself with the special bits and pieces - the fishing tackle, rods, lines, reels, flies and so on, the various bags and boxes, the all-weather gear, the camera equipment, binoculars, field guides for identifying birds - all the things that are particular to those hobbies and which you need to have if you are going to take them up properly.

At the same time, my hobbies are still hobbies. When I am trout fishing, I don't spend every hour God sends casting flies at some mark

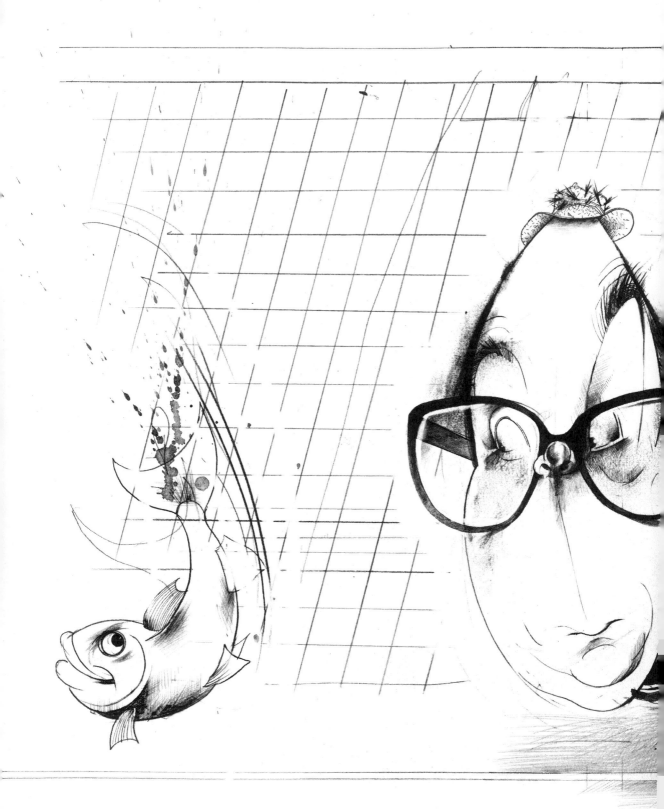

on the river. There is so much else to do anyway, what with tying hooks on, or changing flies, or whatever the moment calls for. But also, all the time, I am looking at the countryside itself, not just in the river but across the river, into the trees beyond, up at the sky. And the more I look, the better I find I become at looking, at understanding how the patterns of nature work together. Anyone who takes up fishing can expect to see some wonderful, marvellous things. Nudists, for instance. Everything is possible.

So, in this book you can expect to find a very mixed bag of memories of fishing as I grew up with it. I have also described some of the things that can happen nowadays on my favourite trout river, both in fact and fiction. It doesn't end there. I have a new hobby coming up fast, which also has to do with the mysterious and fascinating ways of fish. It's my tropical fish collection - a tank each of marine and freshwater fish whose job it is to keep me entertained for hours on end. They are popular with the local electricity board as well, because to light and heat two tanks throughout the year costs more than it does to illuminate the whole of St Albans. However, I like them - Marmite Sandwich, Robin Day and the rest of the gang. I hope you will see what I mean.

ON
MORECAMBE
BEACH

My interest in fishing began naturally because I come from a fishing family. My grandfather made his living as a fisherman in Morecambe (which is where my stage name comes from; my real name is Blackpool).

My grandfather was a professional fisherman all his life, and he died when he was seventy-five – broke. If it's hard work nowadays to make a living as a fisherman, it certainly wasn't any easier in my grandfather's day. He fished for cod, codling, plaice, shrimps – which Morecambe Bay is famous for – and flukes, a kind of flatfish like a flounder which is also special to that region. Some say it is because they come from around Flookburgh, which is just across the Bay. To complicate matters, my father always called them 'skeerback', which you won't find in the average dictionary but I don't think he made it up. The reason for the name, as I remember, had to do with the way the fish's back was formed. If you ran a finger along it from head to tail, it felt smooth; from tail to head, it was rough.

When I was about nine or ten, I started to go fishing with my father. He was a labourer, a road mender for the town corporation, and he would supplement his income in two ways. He used to fish, partly for the family larder and partly in order to sell some of his catch privately. It was never a great commercial enterprise. Relatives are relatives the world over, and ours were typical. 'Oh yes,' they'd say. 'Well, here's a shilling, George, for those forty-eight fish. Get yourself a pint.'

He also used to go golfballing. That meant scouring the local golf
course for lost balls which he then sold back to the pro. As I grew old
enough to help out, it was natural for me to go with him on these
various expeditions.

The fishing was done on the beach at Morecambe. We used to
follow the tide out, walking across the sand until we were about a
quarter of a mile from the promenade. There my father picked a likely
stretch of sand and drove in a line of three wooden stakes, each about
ten yards from the next one. Across the top of the stakes he tied a long

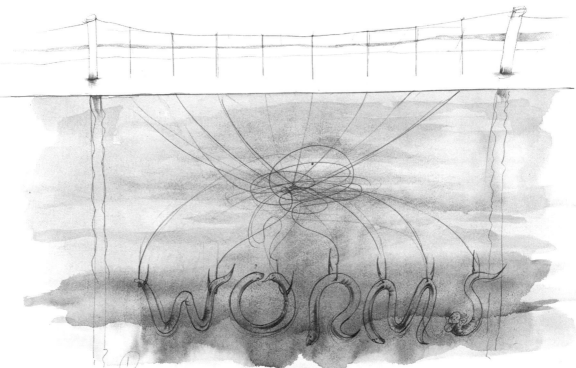

piece of line. I can't remember what it was made of: not nylon, because these were pre-nylon days; it looked like thin rope, and it was certainly seaworthy. From this line, he suspended a row of shorter lines, about one foot apart, that reached almost to the sand and had a hook on the end to which he fixed a worm. So now we had a kind of palisade of fishing lines, all baited and ready.

The principle was that while my father and I were fixing up these 'trot lines', as they were called, the tide went right out and eventually turned. When we had done our work we went back to wait for the next tide, which we followed out again, just like the one before. Only now, on these hooks we had rigged up, hung codling, cod, flukes, plaice . . . On a good day, as the tide inched its way down the wooden stakes, dozens of sparkling fish would be uncovered.

As soon as we could, we splashed down the line gathering our catch in a big net. When we had got them all in, we dismantled the stakes and trot-lines and set off across the sands for home. My father, who was a very solid six-footer, a big 'gentle giant' of a man, carried the net slung over one shoulder, and the stakes balanced on the other. I dashed along behind him with the rest of our gear; I also kept a proud and careful eye on the fish as well – *our* fish.

My father was a versatile and inventive man who would go to tremendous lengths – as we shall see later – to achieve his aims. So, on the beach, it wasn't long before he moved on to another way of catching fish, using a boke net. With this method the stakes were set in a curve and the boke net, which bellowed out like a trawl net, was fixed to them. The routine was much the same as before, except that, as the tide came in, the fish swam into the net which, under the weight of the tide, now bellowed towards the shore.

This technique relied for its success on a known weakness in fish behaviour – they can be stupid. When they are caught in a net, fish don't think of smart alternatives, such as holding their gills in and backing out. The only thing they do is to try and go forward, which of course gets them into even worse trouble.

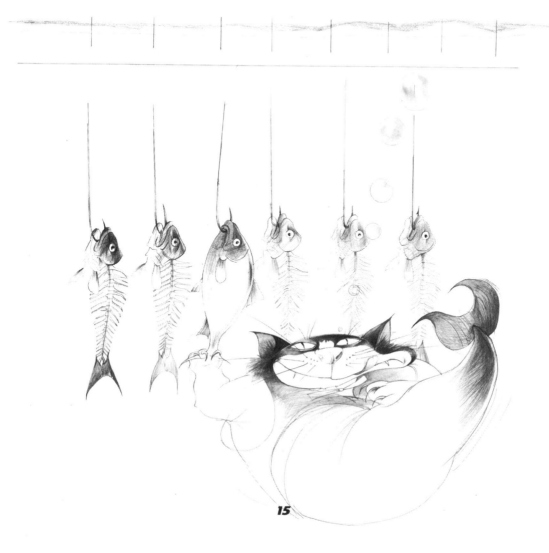

With the boke net, everything went as before. We fixed up the net, then waited for the next tide. We followed it out again, and there, at the bottom of our net, was a heap of very exhausted fish. This system worked very well for us. As a rule the fish we caught were the same kinds as we had caught with the trot-lines . . . until the day we found the salmon.

Below the town of Morecambe, the Bay runs round past Heysham to the estuary of the River Lune, which is well known as a salmon river. This particular salmon, evidently, had swum inshore, taken a left instead of a right and completely missed the Lune. Then it had crowned a miserable day by cruising straight into our net.

My father could not wait. He could not wait to get to that salmon. He had his waders on when he first saw it. He was up to his knees in water and peering down at the net. I can see him now, suddenly freezing and then turning to me:

'Bloody 'ell Eric,' he shouted, 'we've got a salmon in eer!'

Immediately he started wading after it. I could see the danger. Of course I could. I was aged twelve and sensible.

'It's all right, Dad,' I called out to him. 'You can leave it. The tide's got to go out anyway. Why don't you leave it?'

'No, no,' shouted Father. 'I'll get it. I'll get it now.'

All he needed to do was simply put his fingers in the salmon's gills and bring it out. Instead, he went for the big embrace. He seized the salmon in his arms and was about to give it a proper hug when the salmon decided it was time to make a move. It shot itself up in the air, over the top and into the water. Off it went, like an arrow, away to the Irish Sea.

Right behind it was my father. In his waders. He could not swim, but something in his brain just refused to accept that the salmon had escaped. He ploughed on, but with each step fell further and further behind the salmon, which shortly vanished. As it did so, Father slowed down and switched to a verbal attack. From where I stood, on dry sand, words floated back to me on the sea breeze that I had never even heard before.

My real interest in fishing began at that moment. Suddenly I was through with being a fisherman's assistant. I wanted to be the real thing. I thought to myself: 'Flamin' 'eck! I could do better than him!'

THE GREAT INVENTOR

In my childhood the fishing activities that went on in my family were many and varied. It was hardly surprising. There we all were in a seaside town surrounded by a vast bay with millions of fish swimming about in it, and a beach that stretched for miles in either direction.

Morecambe Bay, in fact, goes all the way round to Barrow, and at certain times of the year you can walk the ten or so miles across to Grange-over-Sands. That is, if you want to commit suicide. There are certain special channels that have to be followed. Nowadays the council (if you remember to ask them) insist that an official guide goes along with anyone wanting to make the crossing. Presumably, if the guide goes and misses the route, it just counts as murder.

I can remember several people failing to arrive in Grange. One who did get there, happily enough, was a nephew of mine. He took a pair of wellies and made it in about three hours. He must have been with one of the people who knew the channels across the sandbanks. If you're thinking of doing it yourself, the main thing that can go wrong is if there is a sudden heavy burst of rainfall, which wipes out the channels when you're halfway across. Still, you don't have to go; it's only a suggestion…

Another member of my family who had strong links with the sea was Uncle Reuben. He had a hand cart which he loaded with fish as they came off the boats, and then he hawked them round the town. Then there was Auntie Maggie.

Auntie Maggie picked shrimps. She was, in other words, or even in the same words, a shrimp-picker. This meant that, for some extra spending money each week, she would sit down one afternoon in front of a small mountain of unshelled Morecambe Bay shrimps, which are not only delicious but tiny as well, so the devil to get at, and strip them completely naked.

She would take a handful at a time, and then with her fingers go: chka-tka-chka-tka-chk-chk-chka-ta. There would be bits of shrimp shell all over the place, and at the end of an afternoon Auntie Maggie would have worked her way through a pyramid well over a foot high. And for all that work she would get about…sixpence.

Auntie Maggie was one of my father's two sisters. He also had ten brothers, and they all of them had connections with the sea. But, for me, this formative period in my fishing career was completely dominated by my father who was, in fact, a very special man.

In his attitude towards fishing, my father had developed what I can best describe as a poacher's instinct. He thought that since our kind of fishing was basically free, he shouldn't have to pay anything to do it. This attitude led him to invent all sorts of amazing devices for catching fish, and the fact that nine times out of ten they got him nowhere had not the slightest effect on either his enthusiasm or his determination.

To give you an example, when he went out fishing in the Bay from a small boat, he was the only one who didn't have any orthodox equipment. The other fellers – usually there were four altogether – had all been to the tackle shop and bought the proper gear. They lowered their lines over the side of the boat and watched them go slowly down, weighted with big heavy sinkers. To each of the lines was attached a wire frame, a bit like a television aerial, which had about six hooks on the various ends of the wire. They lowered their lines to depths of twenty or thirty feet, and held them there, careful to keep some tension on them so they did not go right down and just rest on the bottom.

My father wanted none of this. Instead, he found an old bike wheel. He stripped off the tyre and the inner tube, and through each spoke hole he threaded about a foot of line with a hook on the end, baited with a worm. He lowered this apparatus over the side of the boat, holding it by means of a piece of wood fixed to the axle, and let it go down about three feet. There the tide got hold of it. If you looked over the side, you would see Father's worms and hooks whirling round and round on their lines, like dobbins in a fairground carousel. They only wanted the music to bring the whole thing alive.

It may have looked ridiculous, even been ridiculous, but you could not say anything to him – at least I couldn't, not at my age. In any case, he would not have taken any notice. He was very attached to his roundabout wheel. He never caught a single thing with it, and I think he used it every time he went out fishing in a small boat.

Meanwhile, the other fellers were hauling in fish by the dozen, and at the end of the day one of them might look at the empty space around my father and say: 'Oh, and here's one for you, George.' A sad tale, but

Father would not see sense. He stuck to his carousel and, just as faithfully, his carousel let him down every time he used it.

He had more success with birds. In the garden, he took a long piece of horsehair, anchored it to a stick and laid it on the grass with a hangman's noose in one end. He prepared ten or twelve of these traps at a time, then he baited the nooses with bread.

Although this was one of his more practical inventions, it had a

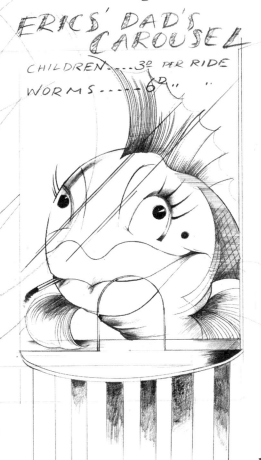

ERICS' DAD'S CAROUSEL

CHILDREN....3º PER RIDE

WORMS....6º .. ..

weakness. He could only use it to catch birds that walked. Birds that moved across the ground by hopping, rather than walking, just came bob-bob-bobbing along…into the noose…bread in the beak, and bobbed off again. Starlings, however, and other non-bouncing birds used to get their claws hooked under the horsehair noose; if they then tried, as they always did, to pull away, they were trapped, because the noose was staked and their only chance was to break the horsehair and this, regrettably, was too much for a starling to do.

This is all terrible to relate, of course, in our more enlightened and caring times, and not the least bit funny, but my father used to catch two or three dozen birds in the course of one of his hangman's sessions. He then killed the lot and took them round to my Auntie Maggie, who had a passion for them. With her it was 'Four-and-twenty starlings baked in a pie', rather than blackbirds. No-one else ate the birds, only Auntie Maggie; which is just as well, really, because a starling, once you've taken its feathers off, has a body about as big as a thimble. Auntie Maggie, on the other hand, was not small.

THE MAN IN THE LUNE

Although I cannot claim him as a relative, the Man in the Lune was a good friend of my father; what's more, they went to school together. So there was something of a bond, even if he was not 'family'.

The River Lune at its mouth is a broad estuary and used to be a busy shipping area back in the nineteenth century. Before that, Captain Cook sailed from these waters, and further upstream, in Lancaster, you can still see the old Custom House. Now the main channel is narrow, although they do get some heavy spring tides which sweep in fast over the saltings – and God help you if you get in the way.

In a riverside pub in Lancaster they have photographs on the wall which show the tide up to people's necks in the bar. (For about half an hour that day the landlord couldn't hear anybody ordering.) It is a fisherman's pub, and my father used to take me down there occasionally – not to fish, because it cost money on the Lune and at that time we only fished where it was free. I would sit outside in the garden holding a glass of shandy, and with any luck the tide would be running and this amazing man would be there.

He stood in the Lune up to his waist. His arms were stretched out wide, and horizontal with the water, and in each hand he held a piece of wood. These were the handles of two boke nets which swelled out beneath in the fast-moving river. He stood there looking crucified for as long as the tide was running, waiting for salmon to hurl themselves into his nets.

I have seen him catch fifteen-pound salmon with this method. When he had got one, he lifted it out, whacked it with a huge priest which he also kept about his person, then he waded to the bank, laid the fish out on the pub lawn, and went back to try for another. He might, on the other hand, stand in the river for hours and get nothing. Stiff as a scarecrow. Then suddenly a salmon would swim into the net. The Man in the Lune's entire body convulsed for a second or two as he fought against the shock. Then he had it. Lifted it up out of the net, thumped it, waded over to the bank. Back for more.

He was a truly astonishing man. A kind of piscatorial Desperate Dan. How he kept it up, I shall never know. All I do know is that you could never shake hands with him because his arms wouldn't come round to the front. But I have been there on days when he took half a dozen salmon in one session. And at six or seven shillings per pound of fish that wasn't bad business. I have since wondered if he wasn't really an Indian fakir rather than a strong man from Morecambe. All that arm torture, muscle ache, not to speak of the rising damp. How can it have been worth it? That, of course, is one of the mysteries of fishing.

END OF THE PIER SHOW

Those trot lines and boke nets that we spread across the beach were effective enough, but to my ambitious eyes they seemed like bucket-and-spade stuff compared with the 'real' fishing that people did on the Central and West End Piers. By the age of twelve I wanted to be up there too, fishing with my own pole.

Even the boat fishing we did was not really skilful - more a matter of 'chuck and chance'. Except for my father who, with his carousel, stood no chance! Anyhow, when I mentioned to him about going on the pier he said yes, he'd take me, and so we made our preparations.

The question of expense, which might have arisen, was fortunately avoided in two ways. My father made the poles himself, so we did not have to buy them. They were literally trees, which he smoothed down a bit and drilled with holes to carry the line. Getting on the piers might also have been a stumbling block but for my mother. She, by great good fortune, had a job on one of them as an usherette. This entitled her to a pass, and for complex technical reasons I cannot remember my father and I somehow got on for nothing, whereas lesser people with no clout in these circles had to pay threepence.

Bait, too, was free. We went down on the beach and dug our own ragworms. At least, my father dug them and I picked them up, and in the process banished for ever any fear I may have had of worms. Not that anyone wanting to take up fishing would get very far if he couldn't pick up a maggot or a worm. Snakes, on the other hand, I am less keen about...

Before we leave the beach and go back on the pier, I would like to pay tribute to an even more delightful form of animal life that lives down there beneath the sand - the cockle. Occasionally, when my father and I had a few minutes to wait for the tide, we would go cockling. This was perhaps the most basic form of seafood gathering that I ever went in for, because all you have to do is walk to where you think the cockles are, and tread hard with your welly on the wet sand. If you've got it right, there is a soft 'schloik' sort of noise - and up comes a cockle.

We used to catch hundreds of them. They are in fact very responsive to the welly-in-the-sand method. For them it must be like answering the telephone. No sooner have you trod down, then, if there was a cockle within earshot... 'Schloik', up he'd come to see what was happening. What then happened was that you put him in your bucket, took him home and ate him. Delicious.

Now, back to the virile stuff. Down at the end of the pier a regular gang of people gathered to fish. There were the old boys – men past retirement age – and the Dads and their young sons aged twelve to fourteen or thereabouts. The only age-group missing was what used to be called youth: the older teenagers and twenty-year-olds, who were more interested in dancing and getting after the girls.

Some of the finest moments of my childhood were spent on the

piers at Morecambe. I loved every minute of it.
Of course, the hours you fished depended entirely on the
tides, and one of the greatest thrills was getting up early at, say, five
o'clock, going down to the kitchen in the dark for a bacon sandwich,
then setting off for the pier on the crossbar of Dad's bike. We had all the
poles and fishing gear on the bike, and our way was lit by a little lamp
which threw a pale yellow light about an inch.

Once you were there you could fish the tide in and fish it out again. You could stay for six hours if there was no need to go off to work or school. You could take food and have a picnic. See the sun come up, feel its warmth. Marvellous times. Still to this day it gives me a thrill, when I go home to Morecambe, to walk along the pier and say: 'I used to fish here with my father.' That is a very special memory.

The most popular places to fish on the pier were round where the main columns went into the sand. Down there were fairly deep, still pools, regularly stocked with a million breadcrumbs. The fish seemed to like these pools, and above them there was always a cluster of poles stuck out over the railings.

One thing you could always depend on: no matter what time you got to these favourite places, someone would always be there before you. It didn't matter if you stayed up all night, you would never be first. Not that this was necessarily important. If the day went well, you could come away with a sackful of fish, and it didn't seem to matter where you sat. On other days, you might get nothing.

It is one of the strange things about fishing that you can enjoy a really good day out and still end up with nothing to take home. It is even stranger if you consider that most fishermen are competitive creatures. They want to succeed, and the one definition of success they all recognize is – fish in the bag. My father, I know, would be upset if both of us came away from a day on the pier having caught nothing. He could even be quite upset if one of us came away with nothing – particularly if it was him. But the irritation never lasted for long, and never kept him from going the next time.

Funnily enough – and this must be a family characteristic – he was keen enough to fish for hours on end several times a week, but he never wanted to go in for competitions. They held plenty on the pier, but he never felt he wanted to enter.

Today I feel very much in agreement with him. Because the word has somehow got round that I like to fish, people and sponsors send me invitations to take part in their matches. I always refuse. (If any sponsors are out there reading this book – you see? I told you there was no need to feel offended. The invitation card was lovely, but I simply don't go in for competitions.)

It is less easy to explain why. I have great admiration for the people who get out there along the rivers and the canal banks. I like to see them do it, and I have seen some fine contests. But for me, no. Especially now that I concentrate almost entirely on trout fishing, which I see as a contest between one man and one fish, I don't feel that competing to catch quantities of fish is part of the sport that I am involved with.

THE BOMB FLOAT

Being a sort-of poacher, as my father was, meant that he was forever on the lookout for other ways to catch fish. If he was blocked by one particular approach, he would draw back, look around for another way of overcoming his difficulty, and charge in again.

How to throw a worm fifty yards across the Lune at Lancaster was very typical of the problems he would try and conquer. And it *was* a problem. Fifty yards is a long way to throw a worm, which after all is just about weightless. But that was where he wanted to drop his worm, on the far side of the river; nowhere else would do.

At last one day he was ready with his solution. He took a worm and put it on the hook. Then he added a float – but this was no ordinary float. Father had been shopping. He had gone to the grocer's, and there he had bought one of those Squeezee Lemons; he took out all the juice and three-quarters filled it again with water, then screwed the top back on and tied it to the line. Now he had a float which looked like a hand grenade and was about the same weight as a cricket ball.

The first time Father tried it out, he was using a whippy river rod. He made his cast and the float whizzed out over the water, missed the river and landed on the far bank. Father couldn't pull it back, it was stuck. He had to break his line. But he didn't give up. He insisted on giving his heavy-water float a full and proper series of trials, which lasted for several years, at the end of which he still had not caught a single fish with it.

Personally, I am not surprised that the fish were driven off rather than attracted by Dad's bomb float. To start with, the noise it made when it thwacked down on the surface of the water would have been enough to frighten every living thing away for about two weeks. Any fish seeing that bomb coming over – and at the top of its trajectory it must have been twenty feet up – can only have thought: 'Bloody 'ell! I'm off.' And you can't blame it. If you had been a fish, in similar circumstances, what would you have done? Exactly.

One other device that became a minor obsession with my father was an American lure which I brought back from the United States. Over there they have different fish and different ways of catching them. They go in more for heavy hardware in the form of big exotic lures that weave about in the water. One year I brought one of these lures back as a present for my father. It had a plastic body with big eyes on the front, and to activate it you first had to split it open and then load it up with a powder, rather like Epsom Salts. You clicked it shut and put it in the water, then the salts did their work and the lure used to fizz about all over the place, erupting gently as it went, like a certain well-known politician after four curries.

Father was delighted. He took it out again

and again. Unfailingly, it let him down. It was the same story as the blomb float, and the bike wheel before that. He never caught a single thing with it. But that never seemed to fluster him. He was happy with it, and if he was happy with something he remained loyal to it, regardless of what other people thought.

I used to watch him fishing with that Epsom Salts contraption and I would fall about laughing.

'Look, Dad,' I'd say, 'why don't you try something else, that other lure I got you, or that one in the drawer?'

'Oh, no. No,' he'd say, 'this one will do me nicely.'

The truth of it was, he would not use some of his fishing gear, especially the more expensive stuff, because he was frightened of losing it. Frightened it might sink, or get caught in a clump of reeds, or just disappear. So he kept this equipment in drawers and boxes around the house, where it was safe. Do you know anyone like that? Yes, I believe there's a lot of it about. I can't see the point in it myself, hiding stuff away all over the house so it won't get lost. I ask the bank to look after mine.

HIS LAST SALMON

I wish I had been able, in his final years, to get my father more involved in trout fishing, which by then had become my speciality. He did have a few tries at it, but unfortunately his sight was failing and he was virtually blind for the last two years of his life.

His great ambition was still – as it had been that day on the beach with the boke net – to catch salmon. He only ever caught one, a seven-pounder, so he still had the will to catch them even after his blindness made it impossible for him to go out on his own. In those last years I used to go up to Morecambe to see him, and drive him to the banks of the Lune and park beside the river so that he could hear the sound of the water.

I would leave him, with the car windows wound down, and go and fish nearby for half an hour or so, then come back empty-handed and say: 'I got nothing, Dad.'

'No,' he'd say, 'you never bloody did, did you.'

Later he had an operation which partly restored his sight, but then unfortunately he had a stroke which, although mild, was still a stroke, and so a considerable handicap. I used to go and see him at the house in

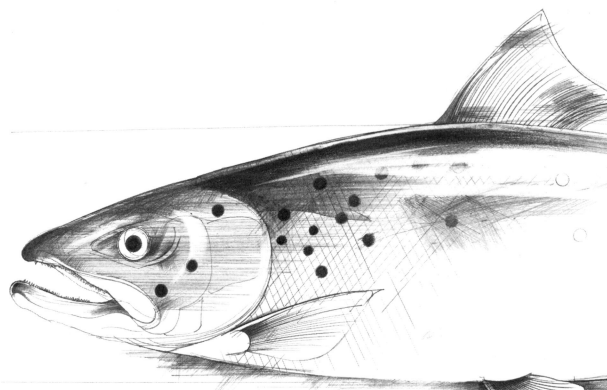

Hest Bank and we would hold long conversations. It was
wonderful that he was able to speak as clearly as he did, with
no slurring. The level of the conversation was not particularly great,
and my mother and I talked to him not as people in full health talk, in
order to exchange ideas and information, but really to keep him occupied
and interested. He could say who he was and where he lived, and we
could even ask him whether So-and-so should play for England and
eventually get him to name a complete team.

That was roughly the range of things we could talk about. But
there was one obstacle he could not get over. If he said something, and
you had not quite heard him properly, and said 'Pardon?' he would be
completely thrown because he could not remember what he had just
said. He would say: 'Aaah?' and sit there looking dazed and old until you
restarted the conversation. And that is how he remained until the end:
lucid in some ways, confused in others.

The last time I saw him he was more confused than lucid, and it led
to one of those weird dialogues that you might think only happen in the
more strange kind of stage play. He came into the sun room, looked
across in my direction and said: 'Where is it?'

I said: 'Where's what?

He said: 'That twenty-five pound salmon.'

I looked across at my mother and she shrugged her shoulders and pulled a face; she didn't know what he was talking about.

I said: 'I didn't go fishing, Dad. And I didn't catch anything. I've been here all the time with you.'

He said: 'Where's the fish?' He wasn't giving up easily. He went on: 'I've felt around in the freezer, and it's not in there. Is it in the back of your car?'

I said: 'No. I haven't got it. I didn't catch anything.'

'Well,' he said, looking a bit cross, 'if that's your attitude, and you don't want me to have it, that's the way it's going to be.'

Then for twenty minutes or more he went on and on about this salmon. He would not accept that I did not have it; he was convinced that for some reason I had caught a salmon and was keeping it from him. I wish I could have said: 'Yes, Dad, I've got three in the car for you,' and given them to him. But I couldn't. There were no fish. And where, in any case, do you rustle up a twenty-five pound salmon at five minutes' notice?

It was our last conversation. I went back to London and within a week I heard from my mother that he was dead. To the end, I will always remember, we had talked about fishing.

HOOKED AGAIN

At the age of thirteen I went to work. I got my first professional job in show business, and the amount of time available for fishing was soon restricted. I still went home to Morecambe when I wasn't working, and in those days I wasn't working quite a lot of the time. So I continued going fishing with my father every so often for a few more years. But by the time I was eighteen (slow developer?) I regarded the Central Pier as a place to go dancing rather than pole fishing, and that phase in my life came to an end.

That was during the war, and by 1945 I had become an ex-fisherman. My father kept it up for a few more years, going out with a couple of friends, but then one of them died young and after that my father went out much less often. Really, I had been his main source of company, and once I packed it in he also rather lost his appetite for it – though he became keen again later. Also, there was a bit more money coming in for the family, and there was less need for him to go out 'commercially' – to get free fish for his own family and sell the surplus round the neighbourhood.

For me, the 'Lost Years' lasted until about 1949. Then I was working with Leon Cortez, who was a popular stage and radio entertainer and also a very good and enthusiastic fisherman. We were appearing in Glasgow, and one day he said to me: 'Do you go fishing?' I said: 'No, but I have done.' He said: 'River fishing. Have you done that? With a fly?' I had to confess that I had not done any real river fishing, and he said: 'Right, I'll take you.'

Ernie Wise was with me, and very early one morning we set off with Leon who drove us miles and miles into deepest Scotland. That day has always lived in my memory. The scenery was absolutely beautiful, and although I did not fish I got enormous pleasure from watching Leon. He made the art of casting look easy – which I suppose it is once you have practised enough – and watching him I was filled with the thought: 'I wish I could do that.' I remember too, if I am honest, that I also thought: 'I wish I could dress like that.'

Ernie and I were dressed in suits. We stood on the bank, me in my brown suit, brown shoes, brown socks ... whereas Leon was in the river with all the gear – the waders, the hat, the beautiful rod that flashed in the sunlight as he cast, and all those yards of line which curled out behind him and then flipped forward and landed softly on the water. It was superb. I fancied it.

NIGHT WATCH

The day out with Leon Cortez was the first reawakening of my interest in fishing. Then in 1951–52 I was working at the Central Pier in Blackpool and got to know two fellers in the band who were keen fishermen. They had found a canal where there were some good perch, and they asked me if I'd like to go with them. I collected some gear together – mainly borrowed off them – and went out with them three or four times.

I was living in a caravan at the time with my wife Joan and our young daughter Gail, who was then aged about nine months. The night before one of these outings I said to Joan: 'I'm going fishing with the boys. I said I'd take them in my car and meet them outside the Central Pier at half-past six in the morning.

'Now, I don't want to oversleep,' I went on, so I (Bighead) set the alarm. 'Leave that to me,' I said, winding it up. I set the breakfast as well, which was a bowl of Puffed Wheat. Minutes later I was in bed, hard and fast asleep.

Next thing I knew, the alarm bell was ringing. I turned it off, got up, dressed, ate the Puffed Wheat. A couple of feet away from me Joan was still breathing gently, hard and fast asleep. I put the fishing gear on – the sweaters, the hat, the wellies, everything – and just before I opened the caravan door I took a quick look at the alarm clock.

It said three o'clock.

Right. It was three o'clock in the morning. But I'd had my breakfast and I was *living*. I shook my wife awake and said to her: 'Joan, Joan, I've got up. I've got up. But it's three o'clock in the morning.'

I said it softly, because I did not want to wake Gail, who was just close by. All the same, I wanted some advice. 'It's three o'clock in the morning!' I whispered. I didn't care if I was repeating myself. 'What am I going to do?'

Joan saw my problem. She read my thoughts exactly. She said: 'What are you going to do?'

I formed a plan. I said: 'Well, I won't go back to bed. Not now I'm dressed.' I decided to sit up until it was time to go. Just before Joan dropped off to sleep again, I said to her: 'Make sure I don't oversleep.' 'Mmm,' she said. Then I sat on the bed beside her, leaning back against the wall, with my hat on and all the gear, a fishing rod in my hand . . .

When I woke up, it was bright sunlight. I looked, and Joan was still breathing softly, hard and fast asleep. The baby was still asleep. I looked at the clock. It said half-past eight.

I went berserk! I woke up not just the people in my caravan when I slammed the door, but people all over the site. We had to sell the caravan after that, because the door never fitted again.

I got in the car, and drove like the clappers down to the Pier. I got there at twenty to nine, and those two men – true fishermen – were still standing there with their rods in their hands . . . waiting.

After I had tried to explain myself, we drove down to a little place near Garstang and that day – although I deserved to get nothing – I caught a small trout, my first ever, on a spinner.

Those outings persuaded me to invest in my own tackle. I went to a shop in Blackpool, bought some gear and got interested in coarse fishing, and in particular in pike fishing.

THE TYRANT

That is what they called the pike in Izaak Walton's day, also the 'freshwater wolf' because of its teeth, and Walton's wonderful book *The Compleat Angler* is a storehouse of anecdotes about these amazing, all-devouring creatures. Pike don't just eat other fish, including other pike, they have been known to bite ladies washing in ponds; a mule being watered in a stream was seized in the mouth by a leaping pike; a dog out for a swim was never seen again. They have a terrible record.

Someone also told me the sad story of the mother duck who was swimming home across the lake with her six ducklings in line behind her. But when she got home there were only five. Yes, you've guessed it. Klompff! And then just a row of bubbles.

As for the things that have been found inside gutted pike, would you believe a gentleman's watch with a black ribbon still attached; two chickens (and they were still fighting!); all sorts of wildfowl; crows, magpies? I don't know where they get the energy. They are also reckoned to be not only bigger than almost all other freshwater fish but to live longer, be more vicious, more fearless, and more difficult to handle.

My own pike-fishing days were not crowned with great glory. The biggest I ever caught were three- and four-pound jacks - as they are known in the early part of their life. But I've seen great fifteen-pounders and they are an impressive sight, especially in the water where they look quite magnificent, cruising along like sharks, or those two-man subs that went out in the war on special operations.

Out of the water, people tend to call them ugly, grotesque. I don't really go along with that. There is always a natural reason for an animal to look the way it does (though I think some of my tropical marine fish go a bit far at times, completely changing their shape as well as their colour - but we'll get to them later). In the case of the pike, it might be an idea, instead of seeing that great sneering face as ugly, to think of it as a lonely creature, a bit sad, a bit embarrassed, trying to grin at someone, to make friends. If you think about it, you have probably got an uncle who looks like a pike. There's certainly one in every pub. Usually he sits on a stool at one end of the bar, and every few minutes throws a handful of assorted nuts into his mouth.

The pike too is a lazy eater, like your uncle, and won't go out of its way to grab something unless it is really hungry. Most of the time the pike's diet consists of dead or dying fish that are unlikely to fight back. They swivel their prey, too, before they swallow them, so that the head goes down first. They know that they can't eat them sideways, so they turn them in such a way that the fins and tail flatten as they pass down the gullet.

I think that is pretty clever, but then I have always had a special respect for the pike. Put it this way: of all the fish that are native to Britain, the pike is the one I would least like to share my bath with.

REVENGE OF
THE CREATURE FROM
HALF A FATHOM

Fishing is ninety per cent dressing up; getting ready. During the last week in February I begin to twitch like an awakening vampire, then for the next ten days, as darkness falls, I make lone sorties to the garage to see if all the equipment is still there, and give it a furious shake.

Back in the house, I sit beneath guttering candles and ritually turn the pages of my *Trout Fisherman's Diary*, stiffening with a hiss of pleasure when my eyes fall on that special day in May which signals – the Off! The green light to indulge my most primitive pleasures for five wonderful months. How fortunate, in a way, that we are controlled by having close seasons. It makes the suffering of waiting that much keener, the ecstasy of liberation so much more enjoyable.

But come with me now into the garage, Gentle Reader, and we will have a little look at some of my collection of fishing gear. There. Close the door, turn on the light. It's all in here, you know. Somewhere or other.

Ah, yes. Now, what is that you have just tripped over? That is a three-legged stool. Or is it a walking stick with three legs? And that part there, which flaps up? Well, whatever it is, last year I used to sit on it. A great piece of British engineering, that. One thing I do know: if you fall off it, you always fall sideways. Over here, by the near rearside wing of this car – which please ignore; don't scratch it as you squeeze past it, just ignore it – are some of my rods. This is the carbon fibre – my favourite at the moment. I've got a carbon reel that goes with it, and they, just now, give me the strength and lightness that I want. Here are a couple of split-cane rods, both very fine. They are the traditional way, and there are those who believe that you should use no other. However, there is no doubt that the carbon equipment has given my kind of fishing an extra dimension. I hate to admit it, but it is also easier to maintain. On the last day of the season, you slip the reel off, give it a bit of a clean, and that's about all. Whereas with the split-canes, it's more like the cricket bat which needs oiling, rubbing down, and all that extra soothing care, otherwise it won't be so good next year . . .

Revenge of the Creature from Half a Fathom

Another thing you will notice as you edge your way round this
historic garage is that everything folds up. Eventually, the fisherman
also folds up. This bottle contains line cleaner, to make your line float
better, and this is fly floatant, which keeps your flies high, dry and perky
on the water. In this box are some flies. Empty. Well, this box then. Got
to be. Ah, two brown beauties. Now, when I take this box out again in
the spring, there will be hundreds of little eggs in there, all with tiny
hooks in them. Here are some more flies; oh, and a packet of Juicy Fruit
chewing gum. These are nymphs, which go under the water and are
made to look like the insect just after hatching. Later (in case you don't
know this) the real-life nymph swims to the surface, its wing-cases open
and it takes off as an upwing dun, and then a couple of days after that it
sheds its skin, changes colour and turns into what is called a spinner. As
a spinner it mates, and eventually dies. For the fisherman, the trick is to
choose an artificial fly that the trout will naturally go for at all those
different stages in the season. (If you are not a fisherman, Gentle Reader,
and you've understood that lot, you're doing very well.)

How nice it would be if I could tie my own flies, but alas the fingers
are not as nimble as they once were. Instead, I attract flies. I don't know
where they come from, half the time. Some of them, I swear, I have never
seen before. They must climb into these little metal boxes while I'm
asleep. When I do choose a fly, though, it's a very personal choice
involving colour, shape, feel, plus, sometimes, a definite instinct for the
right one. The other day I read about an old boy who used to test his flies
by floating them in a full bath of water, then getting in with them and
submerging himself so that he could look up and see the flies from the
fish's point of view. I don't go that far because, as I explain elsewhere, I
am afraid of water and never take a bath. But I can understand the old
boy's enthusiasm perfectly, and his reasons for doing all that.

Over here is a waistcoat. You are probably familiar with the
expression, but I doubt if you have ever seen a garment with quite so
many pockets. Wherever you look, it has a pocket, and by the middle of
the season they are all stuffed full with bits and pieces of fishing
equipment, which is fine except that you can't get into the waistcoat
any more. In theory, it's worn outside all the other gear, by the way, so
that you can get at the stuff in the pockets. These flies here are all
mayflies. They only last about two weeks, but when the mayfly are up,
the trout will go for anything, so you can catch a lot of fish. Which is

why that part of the season is known as the 'Duffer's Fortnight'.

This is a raincoat. And here is one of my father's many sou'westers. This black overcoat with all the cobwebs was his: if he didn't catch any fish, he could always do a bit of busking in that coat. Ah, here is some of the more sophisticated stuff. A radio. If I'm fishing on a Saturday in late summer, I like to listen to the cricket. This is my small bag, which I use after I have set up the main base camp. I put my other morning or afternoon supplies in this small bag, and take it with me up and down the bank. In this drawer are the drinking flasks. This miniature one is just for getting me to the car. Silver goblet. Pipe – ah, I've been looking for that. Reels. More reels. Piece of seaweed. The hamper. Isn't there a nice smell in here? Musty, but rather lovely – a bit like the wife.

Six milk chocolate cigarettes. My son, perhaps? This is one of my father's boxes. Incredible, the amount of stuff he collected. All those pike lures. Ah, here's the miniature television set – mine, not his. If the weather is really impossible for fishing, I might sit in the car and watch a bit of television. The batteries have run down now, so the set won't work. Still, I'm glad I found it, because now I can take it indoors where it belongs.

Over there is a bunch of oiled coats. Two of them are lightweights and that other one is more heavy-duty. They go on under the waistcoat. Really, of course, you don't need all that gear to go trout fishing, unless you are a fanatic. I *am* a fanatic, because I *have* got all that gear!

MATCHSTICK MAN

The weeks pass. March fades into April and the weather is terrible. Every time I have a free day, April showers cascade down from breakfast till dark. Then at last the skies clear, the sun comes out, the lawn starts to dry and I can switch into action. This is when I get all the fishing gear out of the garage and spread it on the grass to give it an airing.

You've seen those three-quarter views they take for the colour magazines, where someone stands in the middle of a huge lawn, grinning up at the camera while all around him or her are the thousand-and-one bits and pieces connected with their trade. Cooks are surrounded with huge pies, soup tureens, cakes, jellies, all that sort of thing; fighter pilots leer out at you from a pile of flying helmets, ejector seats, flare guns, ammunition belts and dozens of those gigantic lipsticks they always seem to need . . .

My version would be more a kind of poor man's *Field* Magazine. Now at last, in the light of day, all those waterproofs can clearly be seen for what they are – rotting. The waistcoat with all those pockets has a spider's web hanging off each one. The dusty rods, reels, bottles, fly boxes, hats, wellingtons, the musty hamper – what a superb collection of antiques, and some of them are less than two years old!

I can't help myself at such moments. I just *have* to put on some of the gear and parade round in it. Over the fence I can see the new people next door telephoning the police ('Big green men have landed'). I give them a cheery wave. I don't care what anyone thinks, I'm on top of the world. It's a wonderful feeling, that. Knowing that a new trout season is just around the corner.

The next thing I do is to have a few practise casts, with a matchstick on the end of the line, just to see that I haven't lost the knack. Actually, it's like bike-riding in the sense that once you've learned the technique, you never really lose it. All the same, it can take a bit of learning, and it is not at all easy to pass on your knowledge to someone else.

I have had no success, for instance, at teaching my young son to fly-fish. I wish I had, because if he could master the art I'm sure he would get really keen on fly-fishing. As it is, he's more interested in coarse fishing. But I find I am only passing on my own bad habits when I try to teach him. Perhaps he should take some proper lessons. I would like him to do that, one day. Of course, he's only thirty-nine now; he's got time on his side.

The absurd thing is, the technique is really ridiculously simple. And yet I can't explain it to my son, or anyone else. And I also remember that it took me hours and hours of practice to get even passably good at it. People say to me, when they hear that I fly-fish: 'Oh, I'd love to do that. But it's so intricate, isn't it, and difficult?' I say: 'No. It isn't. Not really. All you need to do is to get the rod to go straight up in the air, the line to go backwards, and then the line to go forwards. After that, all the other bits and pieces, like judging your distance and landing the fly quietly, they all come together later.' 'Oh.' By this stage they're either still interested or, more often, they've glazed over.

But, however easy or not easy it may be to cast a fly and land it where you want it, you also have to remember that fly-fishing is like any sport. There really isn't a lot of point in doing it unless you want to do it properly. This is a belief that has stayed with me long after I mastered the basics. It gives me no pleasure to catch a fish badly. If I have made a blunder, say I've slapped the fly on the water with a load of line as well, then not pulled in properly and yet still caught the fish, then I don't really want that fish. I take it, because on the river where I go they don't want you to put them back, but a catch like that gives me no joy at all. It is not the kind of sport I am down there for.

In another chapter we can have a closer look at the twists and twirls of the fly-fisherman's art. But right now, it's still early April, I'm all on my own here, I've got a lawn full of grubby old fishing gear and it's all got to be individually hand-washed, ironed and dusted before nightfall, or I won't be ready for *next* year's season, let alone this year's. So please. Excuse me. Thank you . . .

'Joan! Joan! Where's that big stick I use to bang these coats with each year?'

BYSTANDERS

Fishing is not one of the leading spectator sports, and I hope it never will be. There is not a lot to see, after all, and most fishermen prefer to be left to their own devices – otherwise they wouldn't go to all that trouble to seek out remote pools and river banks where they can reckon to spend the whole day unmolested by their fellow men.

Just occasionally, the silence is broken from an unexpected quarter. The sky, for instance.

'Hello?' called a voice out of nowhere one afternoon. 'How's it all going?'

'Eh?' I looked round. There was no-one in sight, either on my side of the river or on the opposite bank. The fields behind me were empty.

'Hello?' called the voice again. 'Hello there!'

I looked up. Way up in the sky, about five hundred feet up, a tiny basket swayed beneath a massive hydrogen balloon. I could hardly see the little face leaning over the side and calling down to me, and yet I could hear every word quite distinctly.

Eventually I called back: 'Hello. Yes. I'm fine. Are-you-all-right-up-there?'

'Yes, I'm fine. Great view up here.'

'Yes. Fine.'

Not scintillating stuff, this conversation, but clear. That was the remarkable thing. I had not come across this before, but apparently sound travels better in a vertical direction than it does sideways or overland. You have to have still air, of course, but on that day by the River Test it could not have been more still. Since then we have had several balloonists overhead, some carrying big advertising slogans. The best was Cyril Smith, flying completely solo except for his little hanging basket; he had the word 'Nimble' written all down one side of him.

THE SHORT-SIGHTED HERON

In my garden is a pond where over the years I have kept various sorts of fish, mostly carp, orfes, tench and goldfish. To protect them from herons I bought a model heron and stood it by the edge of the pond. One morning I got out of bed, looked out of the window and there, standing next to my fake bird, was a live heron.

It must have needed glasses because I think it fancied my heron. It was sort of leaning across and nuzzling up to it. I called to Joan to come and look, and she will be my witness that I am not inventing this. Afterwards I thought: if all herons are as daft as that one, where do little herons come from?

FRYING TONIGHT

I have been unlucky with mermaids. I always get the half that doesn't eat. Not a lot of them come up the River Test, you know. In fact, to see one there, you need a very hot day, half a bottle of whisky and a lot of luck. Then you may get one, but what sort? That is the crucial thing.

I have made a small study of mermaids, and I can assure you that there are lots of different kinds. Not all mermaids, by any means, are the glamorous sort from the seaside postcards, who lure you behind a rock and give you a good time (you may drown in the process, but you always have a good time before you go). Some mermaids are much, much older, and are related to the ancient gods, to King Neptune and all that crowd. Then you have the soppy-looking ones in the nineteenth-century storybooks, mooning about on rocks all day combing their long tresses – and looking suspiciously under-age to me (watch out for Underwater Policemen, they're very hot on that sort of thing).

Other mermaids are said to be actual fish which sailors used to mistake for women. Dolphins, for instance. And skate. Can you imagine what a terrible condition some of those sailors must have been in? They actually couldn't tell the difference between a skate and a proper mermaid. Admittedly, skate do have a human face on that white underside of theirs, and bumpy bits beneath. Even so. Wouldn't it be so much easier if all mermaids looked like Gertrude here?

A DAY ON THE RIVER

This time we're really off. The month is May, the season on the River Test in Hampshire is open, and I can't wait to get down there.

The build-up for all fishing expeditions begins the night before, and it *is* a build-up. By the time I have got together everything I think I am going to need there's enough to fill two lorries, let alone the back of one car. This is not entirely spring madness, there is a reason for it. To get down to the Test, near Stockbridge, takes two hours ten minutes from where I live on the other side of London. In that time the weather might change completely, so I go prepared for everything.

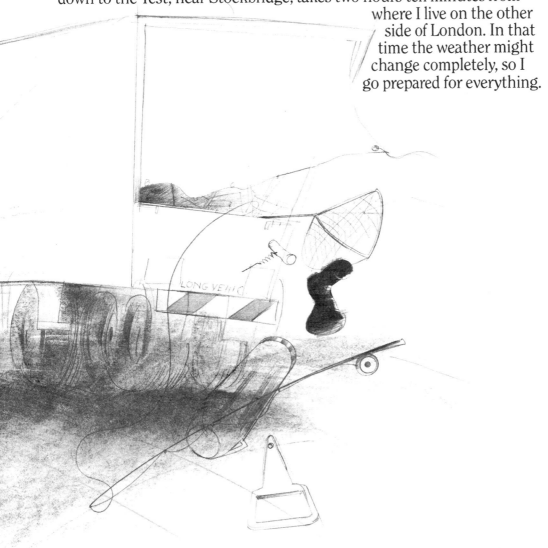

It may be boiling hot at breakfast time, but that doesn't matter. In fact, if it was, that would make me extra-suspicious. I would think: it could be blowing down there, stormy even. So, on a day when you could fish wearing your swimming trunks, I bring the waterproofs as well.

The night before, I line it all up. Check the rods, put them in their bags. I take four rods, and the fact that in the last four years I have used only one of them makes no difference at all. It might break, or get broken. You never know. So might the substitute. Then I'd be down to my last two! Perhaps I should take five rods in future, four might easily not be enough. Then I check the lines and the reels, and the flies . . .

At the start of the season my fly-boxes are *beautiful*: filled with exquisitely coiffured flies in their prime, their bouffant little bodies neatly ranged in rows, their colours rich and sparkling . . . If it wasn't for the hooks, I could eat them – and now would be the best time to do that because by the end of the season those boxes will be empty, or just about. What else to pack? The bottle-opener. That is very important. I usually carry two, just to be sure: one on its own and the one on the Swiss Army knife. The Swiss Army knife has everything for the fisherman: knives galore, scissors, corkscrew, thing for taking stones out of fish's hooves, and the bottle-opener. Slowly I make up my list of supplies and stow them in the big Fortnum-type hamper. The wellingtons (two pairs) travel separately, and so do the waders. Where I fish you aren't allowed to stand in the water, but I take the waders just in case it rains *very* heavily. I don't mind the rain itself, it can rain as much as it likes, but I do like to be well wrapped up.

The fisherman's real enemy is the wind. If there's too much wind, or if it's blowing the wrong way, you can't cast your line. My greatest dread with the weather is to drive all the way down to the Test and then find that the wind is blowing downstream. If I can't fish upstream, I can't fish at all. I can try, and usually it's possible to cast all of, say, three yards. Miserable. In conditions like that, people find themselves going for fish about six inches from the bank – and that sort of fish is not very big.

But back to the hamper. There's no food in there yet, and it's morning already! Quick, nurse, the flasks! One for soup, one for coffee. A couple of cans of beer, maybe, or a half-bottle of wine, or a very small bottle of Scotch and pray that it rains. Sandwiches. An apple. All the pipes. Ready at last. Out to the car. Goodbye, dear. Yes, yes, I will. I certainly hope so. Yes, yes, I'll tell him. Yes, well, if I see him. Yes, yes, yes, yes, yes . . .

I arrive at about ten-thirty. On this particular stretch of water, the fishing is restricted (expensive) and there aren't many people about. Just two or three locals walking about in country suits that make a striking contrast with my circus-comes-to-town look as I unload all the gear from the back of the car. It's all right for them, they only have about 150 yards to walk, *and* they've been at it since about seven o'clock.

Never mind. It's great to be here and now I'm ready for some stalking. Fetch the Polaroids from the front of the car. The Polaroids are magic. Even with a chalk stream as clear as the Test, where you can see maybe six or seven feet down, the glasses make it even better. You slip them on your nose and you're down there with the fish.

Stalking is something I enjoy: it brings out the hunter in me. I take no rods with me at this stage, just walk the bank looking to see where the fish are, and deciding which ones to go for later. It's a funny thing, but people often say to me: 'Oh, it must be so relaxing, sat down there by the river all day. Do you take a little camping stool or do you prefer something more comfortable, like a deckchair?' I say: 'It isn't like that. It isn't sitting down at all. It's long walks, up and down the bank, looking for fish.' 'Oh.' They never believe you. Some people seem to think it's like going to Tesco's. In their vision of things, I suppose, you'd wheel your patio-lounger over to the deep-freeze of your choice, get settled down, make your cast and wait for the fish to hop on to the hook. Well, I have to admit, it *would* be relaxing to do it that way, but a spokesman for the fish has just pointed out that they would need to be dead as well as frozen before they hopped on to the hooks – and they'd want extra money for that.

What is more likely to happen in real life is that I will walk the river for an hour or more, marking out where I have seen good fish or where I think they are. I am allowed four in a day's fishing, and to catch the limit may well take some doing. If, during the morning, I see a big fish, I'll fetch the rods and try for it, but usually I go back to my base camp soon after midday for the soup and the sandwiches. After lunch, I'll walk the river again to see if the morning fish are still there. If it's high summer I may not start fishing until about five o'clock, when it's cooler and the fish come up to feed, and then I'll go through until maybe nine o'clock. Then everything is marvellously still, and you feel at the heart of what Izaak Walton once called 'The Contemplative Man's Recreation'.

There are, of course, miles and miles of books about the art of fly-fishing, but really it is a fairly uncomplicated blend of experience and common sense. There are very few rules. If you limit yourself to fishing upstream, then it would be cheating, for instance, if you suddenly spotted a fish feeding about five yards downstream, and simply swivelled left and cast for it. What you must do is walk back and round, probably in quite a wide arc, until the fish is upstream from you and you can make a proper cast, trying to put your fly in the most enticing position about three or four feet ahead of him, so that it drifts towards him and he goes for it.

.   There are two reasons for walking in that wide arc. The first is obvious: if he sees you, he'll go down or otherwise vanish. Trout have eyes that can see almost the whole way round their head. There is a narrow span at the back which is their blindspot, and if you are up close and stalking from behind, that is where you will aim to keep yourself. The other way to avoid being seen is to remove yourself from view, either by taking cover, say behind a bush, or by moving back so that, from where the fish is, you are out of range – no matter how many of those little dotted lines he draws in the air to try and find you.

There are two reasons for moving with caution is that you don't want the fish to *hear* you. Every footfall on the bank sends out a vibration which, like radar, is picked up by the fish who naturally interprets it as a danger signal. (On the other hand, you can shout at them as much as you like – and I often do, especially after they've just disappeared. They take no notice at all.)

When I was a beginner at trout fishing – I have been doing it for just over ten years – I was delighted to catch all the fish I was allowed. I remember the owner of the stretch where I fish, Bill, coming along to see how many I had got. 'Three,' I'd say. 'Oh,' Bill would say, 'that means you've only one more to go.' 'Yes, I'm afraid it does.' 'Well, catch three for me, will you?'

If I was successful, he would say he didn't want them, so there were times when I'd drive home, smiling all the way, laden with six or seven trout. Today, I am much more concerned with the quality of each catch than with sheer numbers. I would rather go home fishless than with the freezer bags bulging with trout which I had caught by 'chuck and chance'. I can see that it is good for the beginner to have some early successes, even if it means bending the rules a little to permit the

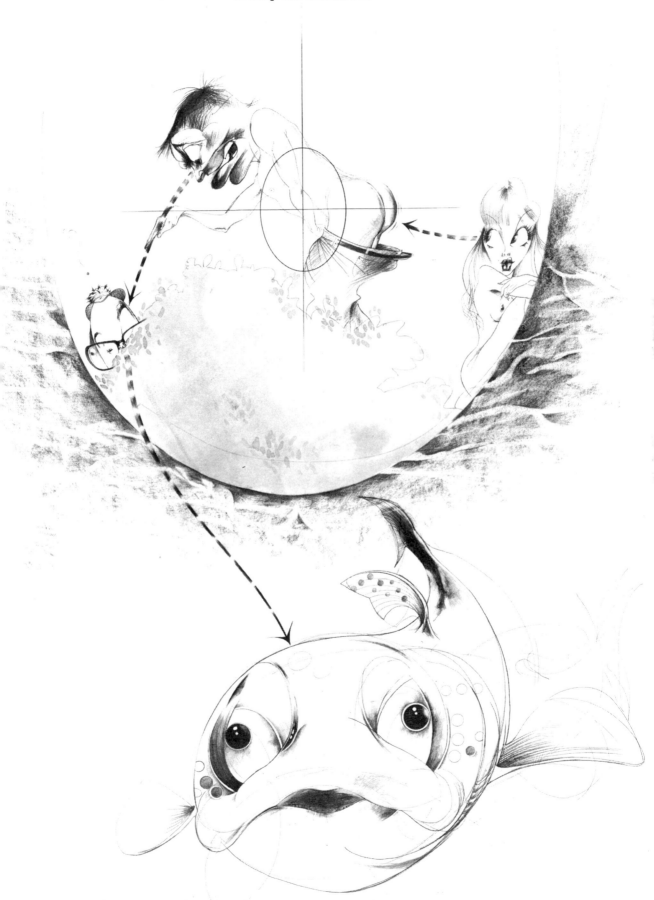

occasional downstream cast. It is not easy to cast well, and until he has the knack a novice is bound to lose a few flies, usually on the bushes or the weeds behind him. So success is important as a way of encouraging someone to stick at it and carry on. But once he starts scoring well from upstream casts, that is special. That is total sweet precision, tremendously exciting – and the end of family life as he knew it!

TROUT SMUGGLING IN OXFORDSHIRE

But before we get too rhapsodic, beware! Fish can pull some funny tricks on you. I was fishing one day on the River Evenlode, near Oxford, where I was a member. My father was with me, and some others, and we were fishing for pike – although the Evenlode is also a trout river. I threw a big pike lure out over the water. It was about three inches long, as big as a small bird, and as it came down in flight to about two feet off the top of the water, suddenly a powerful Brown Trout, weighing four and a half to five pounds, surged up from nowhere and took the lure. Snap! I was staggered, but not so staggered that I didn't automatically tighten the line. I played that extraordinary fish for several minutes, and then I had him in.

Now it was time to exchange guilty looks. The trouble was, the trout season had ended about a week before, and this beautiful plump brown creature had no business at all to be lying on the grass at my feet. It should have been a pike!

What to do? Funnily enough, I did what any self-respecting poacher would have done. I killed it and stuffed it down one of my wellingtons, then limped inconspicuously to the car with it.

Well, what would you have done? Exactly! In your mind you'd have run through all the usual excuses in case you were caught, eg 'Oh, well, I couldn't have put it back, could I. It had cut its mouth very badly, you see. No, I couldn't have done that. Couldn't have brought myself to do that. No.' Then you'd have given it one with the priest and smuggled it away in the boot of your car.

Luckily for me, as I had never been in such a dilemma before, I had my father with me to provide moral support. In his mind there was no doubt at all about what I should do.

'Go on,' he kept saying, 'stick it down yer wellington. Take it to the car. Go on! Do it now. Nobody's looking.'

Covered in temporary shame and confusion, I obeyed. He was right, of course. Nobody saw us. Nobody needed soothing with ridiculous excuses. Thanks, Dad. I think he ate it later. I know I had a wet leg for the rest of the afternoon.

NO FINER WAY TO GO

Later in this book is a fictional story called 'The Fish That Kept Its Head Below Water.' It is about a man who rents the same holiday cottage year after year so that he can go fly-fishing on a particular river; more than that, he goes there so that he can carry on his quest after one particular fish which has been smart enough to elude him and everyone else using that stretch of river for the last ten seasons.

Obviously, the things that happen to that holiday fisherman have a lot to do with how I feel about my own fishing, and especially about the search for quality, and the possibility of stalking, casting for, and catching in one cast a really superb fish. If I can do that – and I have achieved it just a handful of times – I can live on the memory of it for at least a week, with no other visible means of support.

This process of refining the way they fish is something that affects most fishermen as they develop and grow older. As for me, now that I am as old as a can of beans, my remaining ambitions are compressed into one supreme sequence. It begins with me tying my own flies – unlikely now, because the hands are getting stiff, but no matter, this is Dreamland. Then I go down to the river. It is a perfect summer day. I stalk the bank and find this mesmerizingly beautiful Brown Trout. I cast for it, the fly lands spot on, and this magnificent fish slowly, inexorably (whatever that means) rises through the gin-clear water and takes it. I play my superb prize, reel it in, take a long wondering look at it, and fall dead in the water.

What better way could there be of making sure that you arrive at the Gates of Heaven with a smile on your face?

FISHING
ON
TELEVISION

You can't do much to speed it up. Fishing is a sport that goes on for hours, and in the course of a full day probably has fewer dramatic highlights worth broadcasting to the world than the last day of a five-day Test match in Pakistan.

You can't make it funny, either. Really, there are three things the TV people can show you. They can show you people catching fish, or they can not show you people catching fish, or they can show you people not catching fish. Are you with me? That is why, give or take a pair of wellingtons slung in for atmosphere, fishing on television often turns out like this:

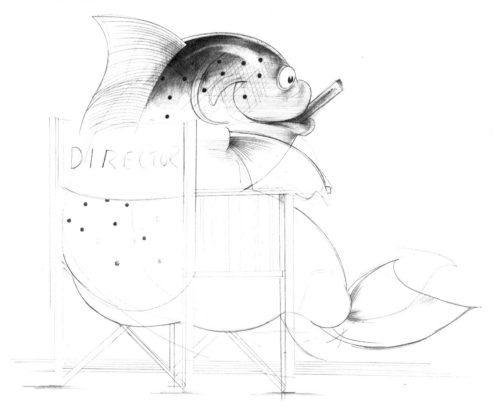

TV screen 1
Head-and-shoulder view of a well-known former England weightlifter, wearing a tweed hat with flies stuck all over it:
'Good evening. It's six in the morning and we are going to fly-fish for trout on the River Itchen.'

TV screen 2
Establishing shot of producer's car outside The Jolly Fishermen, Potters Bar.

TV screen 3
Back view of former England weightlifter standing by river bank, rod in hand:
'Well, here we go with the first cast…
Whoops!'

TV screen 4
Picture of sausage-shaped fingers knotting something:
'Jesus, they've got points on!'

TV screen 5
Ten-minute tracking shot of former England weightlifter stalking the bank. Every few seconds a fierce wind blows his hat off.
'Well, conditions haven't really been in our favour so far.'

TV screen 6
Back view of weightlifter leaning over river bank and laying fish on grass:
'Anyway, here I am landing a handsome four-pounder which, luckily, the bailiff had in his deep-freeze all the time. Isn't that a beauty?'

TV screen 7
Head and shoulder view of windswept but happy-looking former England weightlifter:
'Well, that's all we've got time for now. Join us next week in Ulaanbaatar, when we'll be seeing how the Mongolians do it.'

TV screen 8
Picture of producer's wellingtons. Credits. Music over: Shirley Bassey sings 'Moon River'.

SOME FISH ARE FAMILY

It is one of the mysteries of fish, and of men, that a feller can come home from work, settle down in his favourite armchair in front of the television with a plateful of crispy golden cod fingers, chips and peas, and start tucking into them without a second thought. Year in, year out, he never thinks of changing what he eats for something more exotic – for instance, the goldfish that is swimming about in the bowl on top of the television set.

Taste comes into it, of course, and here I must declare an interest. Although I come from a fishing family, and did my first fishing in the famous bay of the no-less-famous shrimp, I do not eat fish. Not even the ones that I catch, on good days, down on my favourite Hampshire chalk stream. That is probably, mind you, because the fish and I become such good friends on the drive home.

Be that as it may, some fish simply do not have what your local fishmonger might call 'slab appeal'. Goldfish could well be in that group – a bit jazzy for the British market. Other fish are undoubtedly very poisonous. You have probably sampled a few on your holidays. In Italian restaurants they are in the section of the menu headed 'See Naples and Die'. There is also the question of cost. Tropical fish – which are mostly what people keep indoors – may be worth more than £40 each, and you would have to be very rich to want a dozen of those fried in batter every night.

However, one thing above all others secures the future of that goldfish in the bowl on top of the telly: the simple fact that he is *one of the family.* He is a he, not an it; a pet, not a fast food; he has a pet name (Alphonse, for example), and a posh name *(Carassius auratus),* as well as a collection of needs and funny habits that keep his humans entertained and busy for as long as they want.

I know about this because I have got my own private tribe – two tribes, in fact – of tropical fish, and I find them totally fascinating. One lot are brightly coloured marine fish, and the others are freshwater or river fish. I keep them in two tanks in a kind of little lobby near my

sunroom. It may sound daft, but I can go in there with a radio and sit for hours just watching them swim about, feed, fight, hide, bury themselves in the sand. Each tank is a parcel of sovereign fish territory, and behind those transparent walls the occupants can get up to unimaginable things – unimaginable, that is, until you know them a little, and then their behaviour begins to make sense.

In the beginning I was more than grateful for the advice I got, and continue to get, from the two firms who installed the tanks. Even after you are set up, there are plenty of ways to go wrong. For instance, I might go into the shop, see a fish I like and say: 'Yes, I'll have one of those.' The feller in the shop is not keen. 'Well, you can't really, Mr Morecambe, not with the other fish in your tank. That fish you want is a Grouper, and it will eat all the rest.' 'Oh.'

He is quite right. In the great world of tropical fish, there are flesh-eaters and non flesh-eaters. And when you are going through the books and catalogues, it is as well to know which is which. So far, I have avoided total disaster in the matter of fish-eat-fish, though there is one who is shortly going to be expelled from the freshwater tank for his unsocial eating habits – that's the Oscar and we will meet him later.

There are other problems, too, some of them serious and some not so serious. Perhaps the least of these problems is the fact that keeping tropical fish may be fascinating but it is unfortunately not cheap. I put this low on the list because if you are going to take up tropical fish, you must do it properly. It's no good changing your mind every time the electricity bill arrives.

That is the big expense. Electricity. It has to be on all day to keep the temperature of the tank at 76°-78°F. The tank also needs to be lit for fourteen hours a day, with spells of darkness in between. You have to take care when you put the tank light on, because it can have a blinding effect and my fish don't have eyelashes to blink with – only mermaids and fish in cartoons have those. So, in the morning, when we come down and the tank light is off, Joan or I put the main ceiling light on first and give it a minute or two. Then there isn't that sudden terrible flash when the tank light does go on.

Every five or six weeks I change the water, about one-third of it at a time, and add some salt to the marine tank. That tank has various pieces of white rock in it, which give the fish a bit of street life – including a tunnel to hide in. This was very popular with a Large Brown Butterfly

Fish I had at one time, who spent a lot of time guarding it and would only let certain other fish go inside.

Most fish like somewhere to hide and be quiet from time to time, and my Large Brown Butterfly Fish had obviously grasped this fact of life as firmly as any Blackpool landlady. He spent the greater part of his life doing circuits – through the tunnel, round the rock outside and back into the other end of the tunnel. If any fish went in there without his approval, he'd shoot in immediately and chase them out. The Yellow Longnose, for instance, had no chance of staying in there. In fact, I don't think he even got in there.

The rocks turn green very quickly with algae, but you have to resist the temptation to scrape it off, because some of the fish eat this algae – and good luck to them. However, I don't think their main diet is too bad, and nor do they. I give them pieces of frozen shrimp and cockles, and when it is feeding time they get very excited. They dance about in the front of the tank, up and down the glass, because they know that food is on the way. The Cowfish used to zoom up and down like an express lift.

Cowfish, if you've never seen one, are quite extraordinary. They come from the Indian and Pacific Oceans, like many of the others, but that's about all they have in common with 'orthodox' fish. There are various types of Cowfish, and they belong to the group which also includes Trunkfishes and Boxfishes. What is different about all the fish in this group is that they have two skeletons: an outer box, which varies in shape but in my fish was triangular, and an inner, normal skeleton which is inserted into the box. Openings in the outer box make way for fins, eyes, mouth and gills, so that the fish can move about and steer itself, and it can use its tail to turn on the spot. So, when you look at a Cowfish from the front, what you see is a triangular, flat-bottomed fish that looks for all the world like the head of a cow. It has a cow mouth, cow eyes, and little cow horns on top. Quite amazing. But a Cowfish makes a very friendly and gentle companion – unless you get the type which releases a poison that can kill the rest of the population of your tank even after the Cowfish is dead.

Where was I? Feeding time. Oh yes, I had another fish with very strange eating habits. Pink he was, with lots of brown spots. He would take a piece of shrimp but then, instead of eating it, he would hold it in front of his mouth and parade round the tank with the shrimp clasped there like a kind of trophy. If the others allowed him to, he might keep

hold of that piece of shrimp for an hour or so before eating it. The first time I saw him do this, I didn't know what was going on. The fish seemed all puffed out at the front, as if he had just come back from the dentist. I thought he had developed some terrible deformity, and I tried to get him up to the top of the tank so I could have a better look, but he wouldn't come. Then all of a sudden, while I stood there fretting, the lump started to grow smaller. Gone to lunch!

Most of all, though, it's the general everyday behaviour of these fish that fascinates me. Take the contest to be Boss Fish. At one time the Tunnel Guard I mentioned earlier was definitely the leader of the pack. Then I put in a big brown fish with white spots. The Tunnel Guard didn't like it. He swam up to the new fish and slapped him across the face with his tail. Then he came back and did it again, and again, until the other one got the message about not causing any trouble in 'my' tank. It was like watching the Dead End Kids. What's more, it worked. The new fish kept very quiet after that.

There are, also, some funny movers in there. Not just the Cowfish, who is really an apprentice liftboy. I've got leaners in the tank, and sliders as well. At first it used to scare me, the way a fish would tip over on its side and just hang, motionless, for hours. There was a Yellow-tailed Tang, for instance, who would lie around all day, or lean on things. I'd think: 'My God, he's a goner!' A variation on this move was for the fish to slide, ever so slowly, on its side under a piece of rock. Whenever I saw that happening, I *knew* we were going to lose the fish. We never did.

On the other hand, there was one, a Wrass, which regularly used to go missing, for hours on end. Now, from experience, I know that he just liked to come out for his morning feed, and then go back to bed, which in his case meant burying himself in the sand. But the first time he did it, I was horrified. I was so worried, I moved everything – all the rocks came out – to try and find where he was hiding...if he was hiding. No luck at all.

I said to Joan: 'I've looked everywhere, and he's gone. The only thing I can think is, he's been eaten. He must have died, and then the others ate him.'

The next morning, we came down – and there he was. Large as life and dancing for his breakfast.

As for the colours of some of the fish, they seem to me completely amazing, out of this world. Clown Fish, in particular, have the most

staggering colours. The Tomato Clown, for instance, has a brilliant orange-red body, with a bright white patch that looks as if it has been literally stuck on, like a clown's make-up. Earlier in this book I mentioned my Robin Day Fish. Officially he is a Spotted Panther Fish, but I call him after the great interviewer because he has two white spots on his side which are just like the spots on Sir Robin's bow-tie. But why does a fish want to look like a bow-tie? What is the point of it? That is what intrigues me, and keeps me glued to the tank for hour after hour. Perhaps the white spots have been developed so that an enemy might mistake them for the eyes of a much larger and possibly fiercer fish, and so the enemy decides to keep its distance. We may never know. (And that last bit was pure guesswork.)

Another fish which has me goggle-eyed is the Angel Fish. It's a tiny fish, but it changes shape and colour completely as it grows from a juvenile to an adult fish, so much so that you might think of the before-and-after fishes as two distinct species. There are various sorts of Angel Fish, but let's take the Blue King Angel Fish. As a juvenile it has a symmetrical spade shape (as in cards) when you see it in profile. Its body colour is black or midnight blue with many lighter blue and white vertical bands. The adult fish doesn't look like this at all. It has a more puffed-up body, a bit like an old rubber hot-water bottle, and its background colour is golden with six or seven bright blue stripes running diagonally. The tail, also, has matured from a nondescript little flywhisk to something much fatter and more pompous-looking; again, the colouring is completely different.

Why do they do it? Why do they go to all that trouble to convert themselves from one brightly-coloured fish into another brightly-coloured fish? I'm no expert – as will have become obvious by now – but I never cease to wonder at the ways of these amazing fish from the southern oceans, from the seas that run round India, Ceylon, Indonesia and the Philippines…

THE SHOW MUST GO ON

One afternoon I came back from a short family holiday. Michael, who looks after the house and lives in when we are away, came to the door. There was something of a troubled look about his eyes, but he didn't mess about:

'Hello,' he said. 'Welcome home. The good news is that everything's all right in the house. The bad news is that you've lost all your fish.'

A disease called Oodinium had struck, and in six hours had wiped out the whole of the marine tank. The other tank, with the river fish, was unharmed. To this day I do not know what caused the outbreak. No-one can tell me whether it was something in the food, or something in the water, or why the infection should have taken hold in the way it did.

For two months the tank stood empty. Then we cleaned it out and started again. I bought another Robin Day Fish, a young one about an inch long which will grow to four or five inches (he doesn't cough so much, either). To keep him company I found a fish with a nose like Des O'Connor's; officially, he's a Birdmouth Wrass, and he and Sir Robin get on very well. I also have another Clown, and a mystery fish whose name I had partly forgotten. He turned out to be a Sandwich File Fish, but in the meantime we decided he looked quite like a Marmite Sandwich – so that's what we call him. I've also got a Beak Fish. He's very fine and hardy and will grow to ten and three-quarter inches. Already he's sleeping with his tail out of the tank.

Meanwhile, over in the freshwater tank, trouble was brewing. They had all been in good health and behaving themselves for a long time, right up until the day I put the Oscar in with them. They warned me at the shop. To be fair to my suppliers, they did say:

'If you've got any small fish in that tank, he'll eat them.'

I said: 'What? Look at him. Do me a favour. Two inches long, that's all he is. What could he do?'

Next morning I came down and three of the Neon Fish were dead and gone; eaten. Then I saw the Oscar swimming round with his fourth victim, its tail just sticking out of his mouth. And that fish was as big as the Oscar. Since then the Oscar has done nothing but grow bigger. The other surviving fish in the tank are a lot bigger than him at the moment, but he's catching them up. I'm not keeping him, though. He's going back. Some fish may be family, but not him. I rang them at the shop. They said:

'We told you.'

I said: 'I know you did. I didn't believe you, that's all.'

I'll believe them next time.

A
FISHERMAN'S
TALE

THE FISH THAT KEPT ITS HEAD BELOW WATER

The alarm bell rang in the bedroom of the little cottage I had been renting for the same week in July for the last ten years. A tiny fishing cottage it was, just a long cast away from the river. It was paradise: only me and a woman who came to make the bed and dust around the place. She was the kind of woman who could put you off sex for two weeks – three days before you arrived, the week you were there, and four days after you'd left. In other words, she was the perfect woman . . . when fishing was the only thing in mind.

The cottage had everything a fisherman could wish for: a radio that was so old it could run off gas, an armchair that leaned over at the same angle as Frankie Vaughan's top hat, and a table in the middle of the room covered with an oilcloth of a check design on which some very intelligent fisherman had worked out a crossword for himself to do in the long summer evenings after he had gutted his fish and listened to the news on the radio telling him that Paris had been liberated. There were lots of books on fishing, magazines on fishing, a couple of issues of *Picturegoer* Magazine circa 1938, three of *Health And Efficiency*, and one well-thumbed *Lilliput*.

I had been happy to find, on arriving, that there was still no television set. That would be for the next generation of piscatorial artists. Mind you, I would take a bet that even in the twenty-first century that bakelite radio would still have some life in it. Running the full length of one wall was a small sideboard with drawers that shot out after you had walked past them. On top of the sideboard was a mirror whose glass was the same colour as stew. The kitchen was slightly bigger than the three-ringed oven that was in it, next to a sink that was sinking. This sink had three taps – two were very old and the other was brand-new and gleaming. One of the two old taps gave you very cold water while the other old tap gave you extremely cold water. The brand-new tap belched out some brown fluid and made a rather disgusting noise. Outside the back door, under a lean-to, was a very large freezer. At the moment it was empty of fish, but soon I hoped to see it filled with heavy, surprise-eyed, thick, fat Brown Trout, plus a couple of Rainbow Trout to give to people who were just below being real friends.

I sprang out of bed, dressed quickly and went downstairs into the kitchen and ran the warmer cold water into a basin and gave myself what my mother used to call 'a cat lick and a promise'. Shaving was out of the question, for the next few days at least. 'I'll shave when it rains,' I promised my stubbly image in the mirror.

The very cold water was ideal for cleaning the teeth; it also helped to make your eyes spring open and stay there. I looked at my watch; it was seven-thirty. I filled the kettle, lit the gas and put a tea bag straight into the cup, opened a small packet of All Bran and the bottle of milk left yesterday by Dracula's Daughter. I now had only to wait for a few minutes (fifteen as it turned out) for the whistling kettle to boil, then sat down to my first fishing breakfast. The wife couldn't have done it better; her All Bran never tasted this good.

Breakfast over, I made my way into the Rod Room. This was the same room as the one with the sideboard in it. I walked as slowly and quietly as I could past the sideboard. I was lucky, because only one drawer dropped out. I bent down to pick it up and of course another drawer dropped out. It was then I remembered the trick: you leave the drawers on the floor. In a corner of one of the drawers was a very beautiful fly – a Ginger Quill. It was superbly made. I looked at it for a while wondering if it was some kind of message from a Fish God trying to tell me that the Ginger Quill was the one to use. I put it in my flybox next to three Winged Olives, a few Grey Dusters, six Wickham's Fancies, one or two Iron Blues and Pale Evenings, half a dozen Nymphs, the Olive, the Pheasant Tail, the Black Buzzer, and so on and so on . . .

BIG DADDY

It was time to walk to the river. The weather was almost perfect. I set off without rod or fishing equipment and made my way to the bank which was at most sixty yards from the cottage. It was a well-worn path used by hundreds of fishermen through the years – fishermen who, no doubt, had the same thing in mind as me – to catch a big one, a nice three- or four-pound Brown Trout. It had to be a Brown because the Brown is British. The Rainbow is a very good fighter, and probably ounce for ounce is stronger than the Brown, but the Brown is so beautiful and anyway the Rainbow is American. But, and here I must be fair, I wouldn't put a Rainbow back just because it was American – that is, a foreigner. After all, it has been drinking fine English water all its life – and the water in Hampshire is the finest water you can get; ask any fish.

The sun was clearing what little bit of mist that was hanging about. No sound could be heard except for that of an Army helicopter flying low over the water about a hundred yards from where I stood. I shook my fist at it as it flew by and the pilot waved back. 'Well,' I thought, 'that'll put 'em down for an hour or two, that's for sure.' I reached an overhanging willow tree that cast a large shadow over the water, almost to the other bank. Putting the flip-up Polaroid glasses over my own 'help-me-to-see' glasses, I looked down into the water. Standing perfectly still, I concentrated and soon I could see the bottom of the river, the swaying weeds and the still rocks and the occasional spurt of a young fish. Close to the bank the water was very still, while a few feet out it was moving very fast, bringing all the food in the watery world down to any fish that had made the tree roots its home.

For the ten years that I had been coming to this spot, I had seen a fish tucked well into this bank. Over the years I had watched it grow and grow. I told no-one about this fish, which last year I reckoned to be at least seven pounds in weight. It was also a Brownie. He, and only he, was the reason I came to this same place to fish.

During the day I planned to fish all the river, but in the evening I would devote my time to trying to get 'Big Daddy'. He was almost impossible to cast to as the willow tree leaned well out into the river, and putting a fly there was a lot more than difficult. There had been a time, three years ago, when in a freak wind I cast upstream from the other bank and watched amazed as the wind took the fly and put it in the perfect spot. I had put a long leader on and given it plenty of line, so the fast water wouldn't make the fly skim along the surface and put the fish down. It was a freaky, dream cast. The fly, a Greenwell's Glory, was sitting pretty. I stood and watched it make its way slowly to where I knew the fish was. Only my hands and eyes moved as I drew line in. Then – pow! it happened, just where the trunk of the tree leans over the water. Nothing big, no enormous splash. Just a head, a large head, making its way ever so slowly out of the water with its mouth well and truly open. Soon the fly was no more than two feet away from the yawning mouth of the fish, then easily a six-pounder, and making its way surely towards it. My heart was pumping faster than a rabbit having its first love affair. He was going to be mine at last; next year I'd be able to fish some other river . . . Everything went through my mind at an incredible speed as I held this conversation with myself:

'Let him take the fly.'
'I will.'
'And when he's taken the fly . . .'
'Yes?'

'Let him keep it.'
'Eh?'
'Don't strike too soon.'
'No.'
'And don't worry.'
'About what?'
'Your leader.'
'Leader?'
'Yes, its breaking strain.'
'Good God, it's only four pounds' breaking strain.'
'That should hold him if you play him right and are willing to run after him a bit.'
'Yes, it should, shouldn't it?'
'Of course. Ready?'
'Yes.'
'Steady?'
'I am.'

That conversation was held between me and me while the fly travelled one foot eight inches. It still had another four inches to go before the fish would take. My eyes were now like organ stops. I was so still, real flies were walking over me.

It was then that a voice from close behind me said:
'Have you caught many?'

I hadn't heard him approach, and both the fish and I had been concentrating so hard that neither of us had seen him. But it was too late. The voice frightened the living daylights out of me and I swear I jumped four feet into the air, taking the fly with me. The fish, with a surprised look on his face, slid back down to his home as he saw the fly take off. The fly was now in the tree and, like the fish, a goner. As I pulled the line hard to break the leader, over my shoulder I caught a glimpse of an old man. He wore a black suit with a checked cap resting on his white hair. A white nicotine-stained moustache covered his top lip. He was about eighty, but I swear this: had he been only half an hour younger, I would have killed him. The line broke and snapped back, catching my ear, which made the old man laugh.

'First time?' he asked.
'What?' barked a very upset comedian.
'Fishing!' he wheezed. 'First time fishing?'

I shook my head, not daring to speak. He grinned, showing yellow teeth.

'Don't worry,' he said. 'Lots of people lose their flies. It happens to the best of them.'

He walked off with a stick, the stick I would have killed him with, shouting: 'Prince! Prince! Here, boy!' A dog of the labrador type sprang out of the long grass in the meadow. The old man pointed to the water, flung the stick and shouted: 'Fetch! Go on, fetch!' I stood amazed as the dog sprang into the water, grabbed the stick in its mouth and swam straight over to the other side. It climbed out, shook itself dry and sniffed the ground. When it got the word of command from the old man, it picked up the stick and swam back again. I knew that for a hundred yards upstream, and the same amount downstream, there would not be a rise for at least two hours – if ever again.

Now, as I looked into the deep water, the memory faded. I allowed myself a smile as I thought: 'Good Lord, was that three years ago?' For the last two years I had seen the fish but never managed to put a fly near him. I was now lying flat, looking into the water hoping that he was still there and that no-one else had caught him. I spotted a nice-looking two-pounder who looked as if he was in charge of that particular area, but there was no sign of Big Daddy. I had been lying there a good twenty minutes and was now as stiff as a poker. Being at an age when bending things like an arm or a leg is not easy any more, it took a good three minutes to get off the ground and into an almost-standing position. I walked back to the cottage like Groucho Marx.

I got everything together for a couple of hours' fishing: fishing rods (two), net, three boxes of flies (there were more flies in those boxes than on the river), reels (two), freezer bag, extra line (two, floating and sinking), waterproofs (over-trousers and jacket), creel, scissors, Swiss knife, full drinking flask, full coffee flask, full soup flask, insect repellent, small transistor radio, Sinclair TV set and Walkman tape machine. I put all the things in the car, looked at my watch and realized that it was lunch time. I drove to the nearest pub.

PLOUGHMAN'S CRUNCH

The big woman behind the bar gave me a look that dared me to come and order. She looked at my fly-covered hat, the short wellington boots with the Norfolk jacket and the cavalry-twill trousers, the smart Vyella checked shirt with a tie that had a big brown trout emblazoned on it. She said:

'Have you come here to fish?'

She was looking at me as if I'd forgotten to pay, so quick as a flash I said:

'No, I've come here for a drink.'

She squeezed the handle of the bar pump and for the first time in my life I thought I heard wood scream.

'What would you like?'

'Do you do wine by the glass?'

'We don't put it in a bucket.' That made it one each.

'Have you got a Ploughman's Lunch?' I asked.

She nodded. 'Yes.'

'Well, if he doesn't want it, I'll have it.' I kept grinning as she looked at me. But she wasn't smiling. She never took her eyes from me even as she walked towards a large plastic cover and with one huge red hand took out a plastic-looking Ploughman's Lunch. She put it on a cardboard plate and, still with her eyes on mine, brought it over to me.

'Er, any pickle?' I asked with a smile, albeit a more nervous one.

'Help yourself.' She nodded towards a jar of pickles and a jar of Branston. The pickle jar had three pickles in it that had seen better days. They lay on the bottom of the jar in misty vinegar with flakes hanging off them caused by the constant jabbing of a large black-pronged fork which now rested in a pool of vinegar on the bar, slowly eating through the unpolished woodwork. I turned to the Branston. It was next to the pickles and almost empty. The lid was off the jar and around the top, where the grooves were, was old congealed Branston. Inside the jar was a knife with a yellow handle which was spotted with old sticky Branston. I backed off.

'How much altogether, please?' I asked with only a fleeting smile.

'Eighty-five for the wine.'

'Eighty-five?' I questioned.

'Eighty-five for the wine,' she repeated, only slightly slower and a little louder. 'And one-fifty for the lunch.'

She held her hand out. I wanted to take it, look at it and tell her that one day she would be very rich. But I didn't have the nerve. She was a big lady and I wanted to get out alive. Looking around, I saw there was no-one else in the pub, so like all Englishmen I backed down and paid up. I sat in a corner by a dead fire. My back was to the bar but I could still feel her presence as she stood there, her eyes boring into the back of my neck.

A Doberman Pinscher came over and started looking at me. He yawned, on purpose, just to let me see his teeth, all three hundred of them. Then his eyes left mine and went to the Ploughman's Lunch on the cardboard plate. I was quite willing to make friends, so I picked up the bread and cheese. The bread was so hard I couldn't break a bit off for him. As for the cheese, it was about half an inch square and very greasy. Suddenly it slipped out of my hand and on to the floor, just in front of the dog. Saliva was running from his lips but he put his paw on the cheese and made no attempt to eat it. 'Sensible dog,' I thought to myself. We looked at each other again.

'Don't you feed that dog!' called Moll Flanders from behind her bar.

'We don't want customers feeding him, he's a champion. Come here, Claude.' I half-rose in my chair, thinking she was maybe talking to me. As I started to rise, the dog growled. I thought: 'It's not the cheese or the bread he wants. It's me!'

'Stay!' she bellowed at me. Then, looking at the dog, she said: 'Claude, come here! Do you hear me, Claude? Come here! Now! Come on! Here! Claude, *will you come here*! Come to Mummy. Now! Come on. Claude, you Big Daft Thing, will you come here or will I have to fetch Daddy? Come here at once!

The dog never took his eyes off me all through the commands that were being hollered at it.

'Right then,' she continued. 'Where's that lead? Eh? Where's that lead then?' At the sound of the word 'lead', the dog's ears moved back about one-sixteenth of an inch; when you're scared to death, that's the kind of thing you notice. 'Come here, you old toss pot.' The dog, still with its fiery eyes looking at me, moved slowly backwards, leaving the cheese on the floor. That was when I made the mistake of picking up the cheese before the dog was out of sight. As a roar of ownership escaped from the dog's wet mouth, an unladylike oath escaped from the barmaid's red mouth, and I gave out a dry squeak, the dog pounced hard and knocked me over, then lay across my chest and licked me all over my face.

'Oh, you Big Softy,' said Madame Guillotine. 'He likes you. That doesn't happen a lot.'

'Gerrimoff,' I said, quickly and quietly.

'Don't you want this bread?' asked Mein Hostess. I shook my head.

'Come on, Claude. Din-dins!' The dog left me and followed her out of the Lounge Bar, snapping hard at her heels in ever such a friendly manner. I lay there, waiting and listening to a faint one-sided conversation which contained snatches such as: 'There you are . . . who's a Silly Billy . . . fetch your lead then . . . good boy . . . put that down . . . Down! Put that down! Claude! Put that down! What would the customers in the dining room say if they saw you doing that, eh?' I got up from the pub floor and softly made my way out to the car. As I started the engine, Lady Macbeth came running out of the pub.

'Hey! Hey you! Just a minute.' I wanted to drive off but good breeding and fear kept me where I was. 'Hey! Hang on!' She arrived breathless and put her face to my window, which I wound down a millimetre. She spoke:

'My Old Man's upstairs and he says you're Ernie Morecambe. Are you?'

'Eric . . . Eric Morecambe,' I half-smiled.

'Would you come back and sign our Visitors' Book'?

Being the coward I am, I did.

NYMPHS IN THE TIE

Back on the river bank, sat on a shooting stick under the willow tree, the Polaroids on, I looked at the water below me. It took a little while to work out the shadows down there. Then everything came into perspective. There was no sign of Big Daddy, though. 'Oh, well,' I thought. 'Maybe he's off to some other deep ho . . . hole. Wait a minute!' The famous heart started pumping again. I cupped my hands to the side of my head to stop any light or reflection getting round the Polaroids, and sure enough, down there, about six feet down, was what I had first thought was a log. But logs don't have tails. It was him – Big Daddy. He was as big as ever, or bigger. He looked a good seven pounds. What a great fish, what a beautiful Brownie!

It was like seeing a long-lost friend. 'Hey, how are you, you old sod?' I shouted to him. 'Yes, I'm still here, too. Still out to get you. I've got flies and nymphs that'll make your mouth water.'

If anyone had been walking on the other bank they would have thought they had come across a talking tree. Big Daddy moved his tail as if to say: 'I've been waiting for you, Son.'

'Dapping!' I cried. 'That's all I'm going to say.' He went further into the bank and glided almost out of sight.

I looked at my watch. It was almost seven. I walked away as quietly as I could from beneath the willow to where I'd put all my gear. There was enough stuff in a pile on the ground to start my own fishing shop. Soon the rod was up and a large leaded nymph was on a leader with a breaking strength of six pounds. I felt lucky. I whistled a merry tune as I gathered all the things I would need. I was happy and the challenge was on. As the sun dipped behind some trees, I crawled under the branches of the willow tree at one mile an hour, not wanting to disturb my little fat friend. There was no sun shining at all on the piece of water I wanted to fish. I soon saw him again, waiting, and in this light he looked bigger than ever.

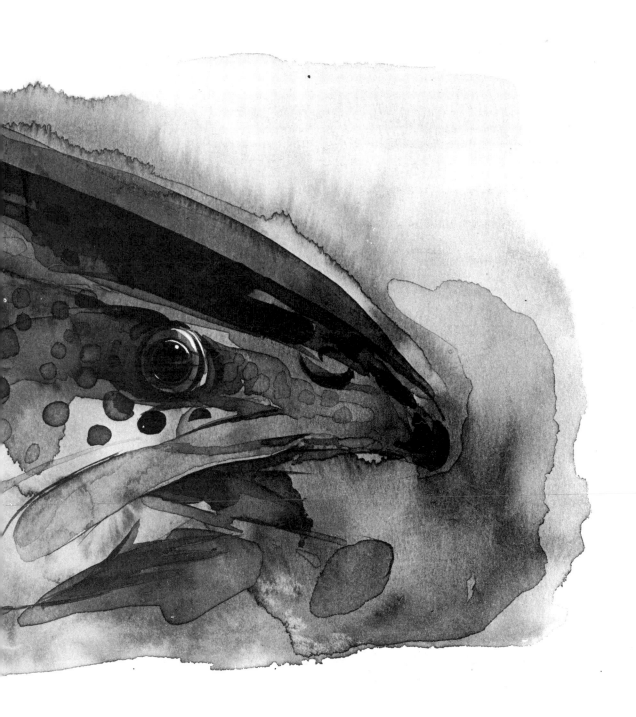

Very slowly and with great deliberation I eased out the rod an inch at a time. At first Big Daddy shot forward about two feet, then slowly, without turning, came back to his first position. Within a few minutes the rod was fully out. I still had the leaded nymph and most of the leader rolled up in my hand, ready to let it drop at the proper time. I was now lying on my stomach. I couldn't flick the rod because of the position I was in. If I dropped the nymph now it would land behind the fish and go further away from him. I eased myself very very carefully towards his nose and hoped that if I was slow enough he might not notice me. It took twenty minutes to get close. I put the nymph on the nail of my middle finger and flicked, using my thumb for leverage. The theory behind this was that the nymph would hit the water about two or three feet in front of his nose, sink quickly to his level and then be carried by the undercurrent to within striking distance. Then, assuming he saw it and was interested, he would strike.

The nymph left my nail perfectly, but I didn't hear the tell-tale splash of it hitting the water. So now the nymph was not on my nail, nor was it in the water. Where was it? It was in the mouth of a trout. Unfortunately, this trout was the one embroidered on my tie!

So then it was crawling-backwards time again, which I did without losing too much of my temper. Once I was outside the area of the willow tree, I stood up to try and get the nymph out of the trout's mouth. After several minutes I came to a different conclusion. I decided to leave the nymph *in* the tie. After all, if a fisherman could have flies in his hat, why couldn't he have nymphs in his tie? I got the scissors and cut the leader, leaving the nymph where it had landed.

It was now eight-fifteen and getting cooler. Here and there trout were jumping. Suddenly Big Daddy jumped. I must be honest, I didn't see him do it as I was crawling back under the willow at the time – but I heard him, oh yes, I heard him. The splash was the kind of splash that the fat guy makes when he jumps off the highest diving board at your local swimming pool. After I had watched the water settle again, I started to crawl back to my position.

This time I didn't go as far as the edge of the bank. I only put about three feet of the rod over the water, but I still aimed to use a fly and the Kentucky Finger-Flicking Good method of launching it. I raised the rod off the ground about six or seven inches and flicked. I watched amazed as my fly (a large Grey Wulf) swept up and then down towards the perfect spot, three feet beyond the nose of the Big Guy. It landed just where I wanted it. The trout saw it all right, and with one flick of his tail swam up to it. I was holding the rod, and my breath, but the old sod knew what he was doing. He went for a real fly at the back of my fly, and as he went back down munching I got the impression that he looked up at me and winked.

'You berk!' I shouted. 'That fly cost me seventy-five pence!'

It did too. The feller who made them for me told me they looked so real that if I kept them in the air too long they could be mated before they hit the water. But now it was getting cold, and I thought the best thing to do was go back to the cottage and make the supper I had promised myself about two minutes after leaving the pub.

Inside the cottage, I soon had the electric light blazing out from a fly-blown twenty-watt bulb. I headed for the kitchen, put the whistling kettle on and set myself a place on the table back in the Rod Room. I was going to sit down to a home-cooked culinary delight – a large tin of baked beans on toast. Then I found out the toaster didn't work, so it became a baked bean sandwich. I ate this delicious concoction and decided to have an early night. As I went to sleep I was still trying to figure out a way to get that big trout into the freezer.

The next morning I was up early, but late to the river because by then the baked beans had joined forces with the breakfast All Bran – a lethal combination. That left me feeling a little washed out, so I didn't really want to cook another meal for myself. It was then I remembered the coffee and the soup in the two flasks. I walked to the car and brought them back into the cottage. I emptied the coffee back into a saucepan and re-heated it. The soup in the other flask still had a little bit of heat in it. I don't know whether you've ever had Mulligatawny Soup for breakfast followed by a dish of soft Coco Pops followed by re-brewed coffee; I can't honestly recommend it. However, after lighting a pipe and having a Kit-Kat, breakfast was over for another day.

DAPPING IN THE RAIN

Once more I sat on my shooting stick under the canopy of the willow tree's branches, the Polaroids on, searching the depths for my playmate. He was there.

'Morning, Fish Face!' I shouted.He flicked his tail. 'Yesterday vos your day, ja? But today you vill be mine, ant I'll put you in da freezer, ja volt?'

He didn't even look up, so I crawled back to the rods again and made two up – one with a sinking line and a leaded nymph and one with a Daddy Longlegs fly with a floating line and a shorter leader for dapping. Dapping is very simple, really. You let the fly land on the water and quickly lift it off again, then drop it again, so it looks as if the fly is dancing on top of the water. At least the Old Man Of The River should come up to have a little look. I had made up my mind to spend the whole day trying to get him.

Soon I was back under the tree, ready to drop and lift the fly off the water without, I hoped, scaring him off, and without him seeing the movement of the rod. Did I say dapping was easy? Yes, but on the other hand a wily old fat fish like him hadn't got to his size and age through being foolish. Hunting him was bound to be a slow process, but at least he was still there waiting. Patience was the name of the game. I moved as slowly as a dummy in a shop window. All I had to do now was to let the Daddy Longlegs down. I let go of the fly and watched it swing over the trout and land in the spot I wanted it to be. It plopped beautifully on the water. I raised the fly off the water and once more dropped it back on the surface. It was great. 'How could a trout resist it?' I thought. Out loud I said: 'Come on, Sunshine. Let's be having you.'

After about ten minutes of dapping and chatting he hadn't moved off, and I had the impression that he was interested in this daft fly that kept doing a dance routine like Gene Kelly in *Singing In The Rain*. Every now and again he seemed to half-rise then drop again. Each time the fly hit the water he seemed to rise a little higher. It was then that I noticed two or three other splashes around my fly's splash, then five or six, then ten or twelve. These were followed by a clap of thunder and a thousand more splashes on the water. It was pouring down outside the tree and Big Daddy couldn't tell the difference between my splashes and the others. The Old Boy went down under the root of the willow and that, for the time being, was that.

I stepped out of the cover of the tree and quickly walked to the cottage where, of course, I'd left all my waterproofs. I was wet through when I reached the door. It poured down the rest of the day, and I sat indoors and listened to the Test Match from Lord's on the radio. I heard Trevor Bailey and Fred Trueman agreeing: 'Thank God we never had to play in such heat.' Fred did actually say: 'It's gunna thunder, thul be a storm afor thend ut day.'

'Do you think so, Fred? I can't see a cloud in the sky,' sang Trevor through his nose.

'Ahm tellin yer, som poor foke are gettin it some weir,' said Fred.

'Here, Fred,' I shouted. 'It's here, Fred. I'm the poor folk that's getting it, Fred.'

I don't think he heard me. It rained for the rest of the day through to nine o'clock, by which time it was pitch dark. Just two things consoled me at the time: Big Daddy had been interested – and there was always tomorrow.

Then, of course, it rained on and off for the next couple of days. In that time I caught three trout – two pounds in weight between them. They now lay at the bottom of the freezer. One of them was a respectable size, one was distinctly small and one was so small it could have squeezed into a full tin of sardines without disturbing the oil.

Soon it was my last day on the river. The weather looked perfect for fishing, overcast and no wind. The temperature was 54° at seven-thirty in the morning. At that rate it would be a very hot afternoon – not good for fishing, but it could be very good from early evening until dusk (all fishermen must think this way). I ate a hearty breakfast that morning, not wanting to take anything back home for the wife. I had two cups of tea, twelve Puffed Wheat in half a pint of almost-off milk, a packet of crisps, two slices of whole-wheat toast with a quarter of a jar of Tiptree's jam, four fish fingers, a boiled egg with a Mother's Pride crust cut into soldiers. It was the kind of breakfast you were never given at home. Then I packed everything in the car, intending to fish through until dark and drive straight home.

I was back at my old place, under the willow tree. He was still there, still waiting. I shouted to him: 'Last day, today, Kid. So make the most of it.' I looked down at him and saluted, like the Red Baron did after he'd shot you down. The movement startled him a little and he very quickly moved to the safety of the willow roots.

I walked the length of the stretch of river I was allowed to fish, intending to cross the old Bailey Bridge and walk back on the other side. I saw a good rise and cast to it for a few minutes, and got the fish on the fifth cast. Normally I feel that if you don't get them by the sixth cast you ain't never going to get them. So it was hard luck for this Rainbow and well done me. He weighed nearly two pounds. Mind you, it was a fisherman's 'nearly two pounds'. He weighed a pound and a quarter. I covered him with grass and hid him, marking him with a stick. An hour later I hooked another good 'un but lost him; he must have weighed a fisherman's four pounds.

At around five o'clock I started to make my way to the willow tree. I had had a good day, having caught and landed three good fish, two Rainbow and one good Brown. If you put the lot together it worked out that in one week of fishing I had denuded the river of six fish – four really, plus the tiny one the cat wouldn't look at and the near-tiny one the wife wouldn't look at. But the three fish I'd caught today were great and made up for the thin takings on the other days. Anyway, I could always tell the wife lies when I got home. That was a fisherman's prerogative . . .

'I gave six away, darling!'

'Who to?' She is a practical lady who has this great gift of knowing when I'm lying.

'Eh?'

'Who to?'

'Er, I gave two to Dracula's Daughter, the one who looks after the cottage . . .'

'And the other four?'

'Well, there was one for the Bailiff.'

'I should have thought that he would be able to get as many as he wanted, being the Bailiff.'

'Yes, they can, but, er, it's not often they get a fish from someone like Eric Morecambe, is it?'

'I suppose you signed it for him.' Here I laugh. I always laugh when she's quicker than me. She lets me finish laughing and says: 'Go on.'

'What? Go on what, dear?'

'There's still three left.'

'Yes, well I gave them to this fellow I met . . . er, in, er . . .'

'Sainsbury's?' Now I have to laugh again, slightly forcing it perhaps, but not enough to show.

'No, in a pub . . . I was having lunch there and there was, er, a wedding reception and they recognized me and sent me a drink over and then they asked if I would have a picture taken with them, so with it being a wedding I said yes and after the picture was taken, and as a gag, I gave them three fish . . . Everybody laughed.'

'I'm sure they did. Three dead trout make a wonderful wedding present. I bet they had them that night.'

'That wouldn't be the only thing they'd have that . . .'

'There's no need to be vulgar.'

And so on. Still, what did it matter? I had a few hours yet to think up some better excuses – I hoped.

I reached the willow tree at five-thirty. I looked down into his watery home. 'I hope you've packed and told all your friends that you're leaving today, that you're going to spend the rest of your life with me,' I shouted. He didn't move. I had a plan. I moved out from the tree and stood about four yards up from it, the rod and line ready with a large Red Wulf attached to a six-pound breaking-strain leader. I cast straight across the river. It landed well out and at the same time I let lots of line out so the fly would go with the flow of the river and I could then work it slowly back underneath the tree.

The fly and the river did what I hoped they would, and slowly the fly moved into the dead water. I tried to guide it through an opening of about two feet where the branches hung into the water. It wasn't an easy thing to do because it depended on the current taking it. The hardest thing to do in a situation like that is to watch the fly and at the same time see if the fish has moved away. You can only do it if one of your eyes goes one way and the other eye goes the other way. Anyone that gifted would be able to watch tennis without moving their head at all.

The trout took the fly very gently, so gently I couldn't believe it. I didn't even see a murmur of a ripple, just a fly on top of the water . . . and then gone. I did nothing, the fish did it all. It took the fly. It put the hook in its lip.

It went off like lightning, the reel screamed, then it came back towards me. I drew line in at speed. It went off again. The only thing I did right was to hold the rod up. We did this backwards-and-forwards routine for a few minutes, and then fortunately he went straight down-river, away from the willow.

Had he forced his way upstream I would have lost him; the line would have caught in the branches of the tree. But he didn't. As he went downstream I went with him, trying to turn him so that he was facing upstream. In that position he would tire sooner. He dived for a patch of weed. Now, the best thing to do with weed is to avoid it. The hard thing to do is to tell that to the fish. An instant later he was in the weeds. If I pulled the line, he would break the leader which could not withstand

the weight of the weed as well as the power of a big frightened trout.

Over the years, if I've learned anything about fishing, it is the need for patience. So, remembering words told to me by greater fishermen than I'll ever be, I immediately let the line go loose and waited. I waited over an hour. Then it happened. The fish was pulling again, out of the weeds. He thought I'd gone home. Soon we were at it hammer and tongs again. For twenty minutes I battled to keep him from going back in the weeds. He was beginning to tire and every once in a while he came to the surface and lay there, then off he'd go again, but each time he went his strength was less and less. He was done for. I flicked the landing net to its full extent. He didn't dive away, he knew he was mine. I put the net under him and, as carefully as I could, lifted him out of the water on to the bank.

He lay there, this wonderful Brown Trout. I had put my hands into the water, so when I picked him up he wouldn't feel the heat from them. I looked down at this great fish that I had known for such a long time. His eye looked at me as if to say: 'Let me die quickly.' One quick hard tap on his head, that was all there was left to do.

I took the priest out of my pocket to give him the last rites and, with one hard movement, I threw it away. I couldn't do it. He wasn't my enemy any more, he was a friend. I quickly removed the hook, eased him back into the water and he went on his side. I leaned over, putting my hands under him to right him and gently eased him backwards and forwards in the water. I did this for quite a long time, with tears in my eyes. The backwards-and-forwards movements were like artificial respiration, and soon he was starting to get his strength back. A couple of times he tried to get away, but I held him as best I could, tickling him in the belly and under the chin. He seemed to like the roughness of my wet jacket. When I let him go, he flicked his tail a few times and then left me. It was almost dark as I took out my drinking flask, raised it to him and said: 'Here's looking at you, Kid.'

I drove home. The following year I went back to the river. In place of the cottage was a new bungalow; the willow had been chopped down and there was no sign of Big Daddy. I never went again.

ANGLEPOISE

The image of fishing is important. There is something very special about the idea of going off for a day's fishing. It's attractive, the notion of hunting beautiful creatures that live in water, and catching them; it encourages you to get going in the morning and later, in the evening, the memory of what you have done keeps you wanting to come back for more.

It's healthy too – it has you out in the open air for eight or more hours at a stretch. You don't do a lot physically, but most of the time you're busy doing something or other – and you can get yourself into some interesting positions; sometimes it's a bit like unorganized yoga. The other main point is that fishing is mysterious. Because of the techniques involved, and the way people go off into the middle of nowhere to put them into practice, the general non-fishing public is kept slightly at arm's length. They never quite know what's going on, or why (and that's the way we intend to keep it). In fact, if there has to be one word to describe the image of fishing, with its intriguing blend of skill, rugged endeavour and remoteness, it has to be... *smart*. Some people, of course, might think that means looking smart. They could not be more wrong.

The truth of the matter is, it is impossible to be a fisherman and look smart. This is not just personal prejudice, the fact that when I am out fishing I look as if I have dressed in front of a jet engine...there is more to it than that. I *know* it can't be done. I will give you an example.

You will have seen, no doubt, plenty of well-dressed fishermen walking about with flies in their hats. Now, I've tried that. The theory is fine: there they all are, you've got them, a complete set for a day's casting, just inches from your hand whenever you want one. There's only one catch. Literally. You can't get them out! Whenever I look at a flies-in-the-hat man now, I think they must be real flies that he's had sprayed on as a special effect.

There used to be a time when I thought: Ah, I'll try that. So I'd load up the hat until it was stiffer with flies than a jam tart in a heatwave, then set off up the river bank. Suddenly, I'd see a fish. Right, I'll try this Ginger Quill. Reach up for it... this Ginger Quill, this Ginger... Impossible. Stuck fast. Give it a pull. Yowp! After five minutes of me writhing about and stabbing myself, even the fish used to get bored and swim away. And why not? When you think about it, the fly is a decorated barb, and the hat is made of wool. And barb and wool don't mix. Even a fish knows that.

In short, if fishing *is* smart, there must be some explanation which goes beyond mere appearances. In the next few pages, you will find some images of typical fishing folk. Have a look at them, and then see if you can spot the elusive ingredient that is still driving millions of innocent people to go, as Izaak Walton put it, 'a-Angling'.

THE SALMON WRESTLER

If exclusive is the name of the game, then this feller must take the gold medal and biscuit. Just think, he is paying good money (very good money) to stand in a freezing-cold river up to his nostrils, fighting to control his rod in a gale and a half while he flicks his fly after salmon. I could never do that. For a start, I never stand in water when I go fishing, and for a very good reason: I'm terrified of it. Speak to me not of thigh-waders, chest-waders, Spiderman outfits. Short wellingtons are what I wear–and they are for keeping me out of danger from puddles on the bank.

THE RACONTEUR

This man is usually encountered on very dry land. He likes the feel of a carpet beneath his feet, a pint mug at his elbow, and although no-one has seen him catch anything for the last seven years, this gesture is still his answer should anyone ask him how he got on that afternoon. He is in fact the son of the man who used to tell those stories about 'the one that got away'. What he is actually saying (softly and to himself alone) is: 'I caught it four feet from the bank.' If even a tiny fraction of this man's claims were true, whole rivers would be blocked, dammed by gigantic fish, unable to back up or turn round while they waited for him to come along and catch them.

I AM THE GREATEST

This man is at least two up on the Raconteur. Not only has he made a real catch, he is proudly showing *two* weighable fish. All the same, he does look a little bit smug, doesn't he? Never mind. If you've got a camera, the answer is in your hands. Just point it at him, look through the viewfinder and keep saying 'Slowly back' until you hear the splash.

THE CANAL-SIDER

This man has everything, including a laundry basket to keep his
sandwiches in, and several boxes of Whiffs. These are useful because in
the evening when he runs out of bait and worms he can always put on a
cigar and try that. You can tell he is in no hurry to go home because of
the visor which he wears to ward off the last fierce rays of the setting
sun. At dusk he has a final rummage round in the laundry basket to see
if there are any sandwiches left. If there aren't any, he knows it's time for
his tea and goes home.

THE IDLER

This very relaxed fisherman is trying to recapture the way people lived in a calmer, more gracious age. Either that, or he should be at school. Whichever it is, he is making a tactical error in thinking he can fish and

drink and lie down all at the same time.
You can perm any two from those three
but, if you choose fishing and drinking,
the trick is to stay on your feet.

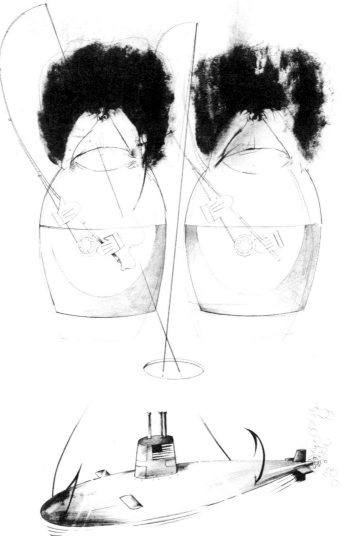

THE ICEMEN

Let's get it straight from the beginning. These men are not like us. This is not the Serpentine on Boxing Day but a Russian reservoir, and these men fishing, and whatever else some of them may be doing through the ice, are doing it in pursuit of a single purpose. For them the main object of the exercise is to catch fish to eat. If you asked the average British angler whether he fancied fishing through a hole in the ice while wrapped in a plastic bag, he might say: 'Yes, I'll do it once. Just to see what it's like.' But that would be all. There can't be any enjoyment in doing that sort of thing. On the other hand, if it was your fate to be born in Russia, maybe you could get to like it. (If our friend the Salmon Wrestler, above, actually enjoys what he does, anything is possible.)

THE WIFE

Its the wife! Not my wife, I hasten to add, it must be somebody else's. My wife has never seen the attraction of sitting for six or seven hours on a hard plank in the middle of a reservoir in the pouring rain and bitter cold while her beloved catches nothing. I can't say I blame her. But there are wives who go as spectators, either to keep an eye on the old man or because he wants her to be there with him (and make up the baits and give him his dinner). The way I see it, you've got to like the countryside a lot just to go and sit in the middle of it for hours on end without moving. But I have known wives who went along and did something else nearby, like sketching or painting for instance. That seems to make more sense.

Going back to my wife – as I constantly do – I wouldn't mind her coming with me if she herself wanted to fish (always provided she never caught more than I did, or bigger ones). If she was really keen on fishing, I would enjoy going with her and we would share all the pleasures of the day out – the dressing up, the journey to the river, then the fishing and the drive home. Unfortunately, we would have to take two cars because she wouldn't be able to breathe with all the pipe smoke I would be puffing out on the way back. As it is, she is not the slightest bit interested in fishing, so what happens is that she encourages me to go – and I do. It's a good balance: I get the 'Yes, you can go,' plus an apple and a pat on the head when I'm leaving, which is a lot better than me saying 'Well, I'm off and I don't care what you think.' I would not like to live like that – and I'm glad I don't have to.

THE LEANER

Isn't he wonderful? Immaculate! Never caught a fish in his life, mind, but that's a lovely suit he's wearing. All those bits of leather tacked on to make him go faster. And the pockets! That jacket must have twenty-eight pockets in it, to carry his various sporting accessories. Actually, they're all empty at the moment because he doesn't want to spoil the hang. The hang is very important. Especially when you are a Leaner, and your favourite habitat is not the river bank or the grouse moor, but the bar.

This is, in a way, where we came in at the beginning of this chapter – trying to account for the fact that fishing has this select, clubby, distinguished image, while at the same time anyone who fishes knows that it is completely impossible to look in any way smart while he is out hunting fish. Well-dressed, perhaps, but smart, never. And yet fishing is surrounded by that clubland aura of oak-panelled walls, Dry Fly sherry, malt whisky taken neat or with the briefest dash of soda, the stuffed wife in the glass case...

Speaking of bars, we have included in our illustration one piece of equipment that may be unfamiliar to non-fishing people. This is the Leaner's Bar, which is extremely handy because it can be carried down to the very water's edge. It consists of a small polished mahogany bar-top, about two feet wide and six inches deep, which is supported on the end of a long pole like a shooting stick with shelves attached to hold bottles and all the extra bits. At about twelve o'clock, when the fish are resting, you take your little bar down to the water... and lean on it. Now that's what I call smart.

Anglepoise

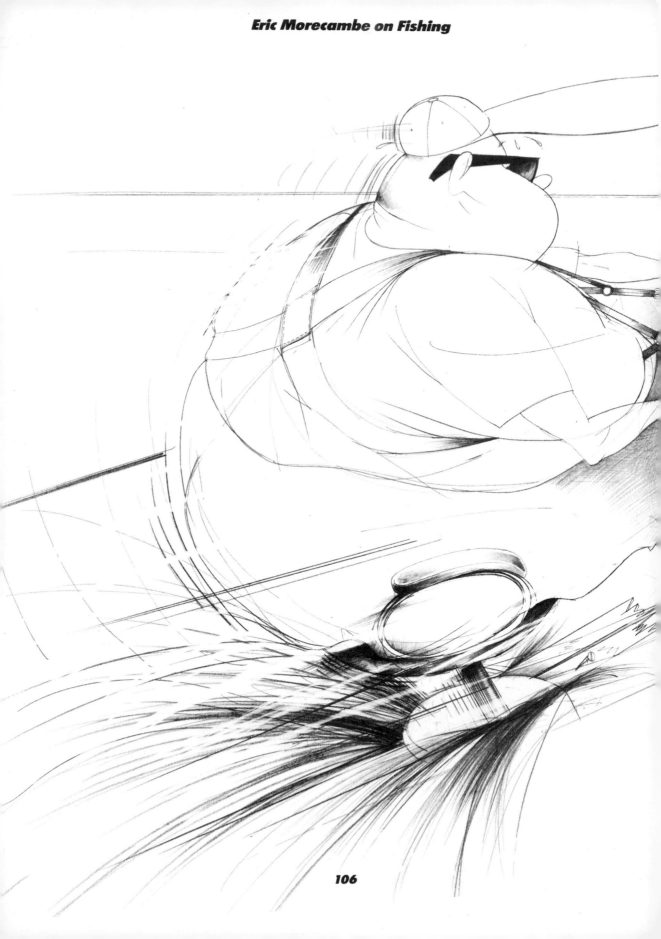

THE CHAIRMAN

Here is something else I could never do: let myself be strapped in a chair and fish for 200lb marlin – on the end of a 4lb breaking strain! If I was a younger man, maybe I would want to have a go. But look at the effort you need to make, just lifting that rod, let alone reeling in and reeling out all day long. It's great in films, though. Remember Pathé Pictorial? They used to get through forty sharks every week.

THE DEMONSTRATOR

This man is not a person, he's a photograph! In real life he was a major-general, then he fell in with a ruthless photographer and for the last eighty-seven years, drugged to the eyeballs on Scotch and opium, he has been modelling the twelve-o'clock-high position for books on trout fishing. The suit belonged to his father.

THE
ANTI-FISHERMEN

In recent months there have been fresh eruptions from the hunt saboteurs, who threaten to move in on our sport and disrupt it. The saboteurs would have you believe that fishing is cruel and should be completely banned. By fishing they mean freshwater fishing – in rivers, lakes and reservoirs. Sea fishing, for some odd reason, is always left out of their arguments.

Strangely enough, I have some sympathy for some of the ideas put forward by the anti-hunting lobby. At the same time, I have a strong feeling that if any hunt saboteurs came barging in on the stretch where I fish, then the shotguns would be out and the saboteurs could well be threatened with a dose of pellets in the pants. And I wouldn't mind that at all.

If I seem to be facing both ways at once in this controversy, let me quickly say that I am fundamentally on the side of the people who enjoy their country sports and wish to continue doing so. Where I have reservations, increasingly so as I grow older, is in the quantity of animals killed and in some of the methods used.

In fishing, I wish there could be almost no killing – but until someone invents a rubber hook I can't see that happening. I don't personally like live-baiting, the process whereby a live fish – a dace, say, or a roach or rudd – is impaled on a hook, or Jardine snap-tackle, and set as bait to lure a bigger fish such as a pike. Fewer people go in for live-baiting nowadays than used to in Victorian times, but it is still an accepted method in the fishing community. Dead-baiting I do not mind so much. If the fish is already dead, then the question of its feeling pain does not arise. But, as I said in a previous chapter, it is the *quality* of the individual catch that really matters, not how many fish end up in your keep-net or freezer-bags. Some fishermen are a little bit inclined to see their sport too much in terms of match-angling, of collecting fish by the bagful, and not enough in terms of hunting for the best single adversary to be found in a particular stretch of water.

What the anti-fishing lobby does not seem to understand, often because its members have no day-to-day contact with the countryside, is that it is necessary to cull certain species of wildlife if we are to preserve the present balance in nature. No-one could manage a dairy farm that had more foxes than cows – and no-one wants a river that is so full of fish you could walk across it on their backs; it's not good for the fish, quite apart from anything else.

In Africa, too, it may seem sad that men have to go out and shoot such magnificent creatures as the elephants. And yet it has been proved

time and time again that the well-run game reserve, with its organized programme of culling, is by far the best means of preserving a good balance in nature. Take away the game reserve, and what you get is the terrible greed and savagery of poachers. Then the region loses many more elephants than it would have done or needs to do, given a properly worked-out system.

Fishing in Britain is well organized. It has to be. About three million people go fishing each year and it is essential that the places they go to are adequately controlled. The National Federation of Anglers plays a big part in this, seeing that competitions are run according to a fixed set of rules and that people enjoy their sport in a sensible, restrained way. On privately owned waters, the bailiffs keep out the poachers – or try to – and the number of fishermen per stretch of water is carefully limited. On that basis, no saboteur or anyone else could really claim that fishing is the unthinking slaughter it is sometimes made out to be.

And what about the fish that are never caught? A fish that can grow to ten pounds in the Hampshire trout streams has to be more than a bit crafty to survive that long, I will admit. But I have seen them; and not only do they exist, they are the sort of fish that keep people like me going back year after year to try and catch them (see also 'The Fish That Kept Its Head Below Water').

There is a political side, too. It happens to work in favour of the fishermen, but it needs to be mentioned in any case. Fishing is a traditional and important recreation of the working man. Plenty of people would rather spend an afternoon on the bank of a canal or a river than go to a football match. Politicians are rightly aware of this, and I should be very surprised if a Bill to ban fishing ever got beyond the talking stage before it was quietly dropped.

Meanwhile, I cannot see how the saboteurs could really mount an effective demonstration. If the land is private, the owners would see to it that any demonstrators were met at the gate and turned off (with or without shotguns). And at a more accessible site, like Grafham Water near Huntingdon, the demonstrators would find themselves up against an army of fishermen. Around ten thousand people go to fish at Grafham every year, and on summer evenings you will find them standing six yards apart as far as the eye can see. Try anything funny with that lot, and my guess is that the anti-fishermen would end up *in* Grafham Water.

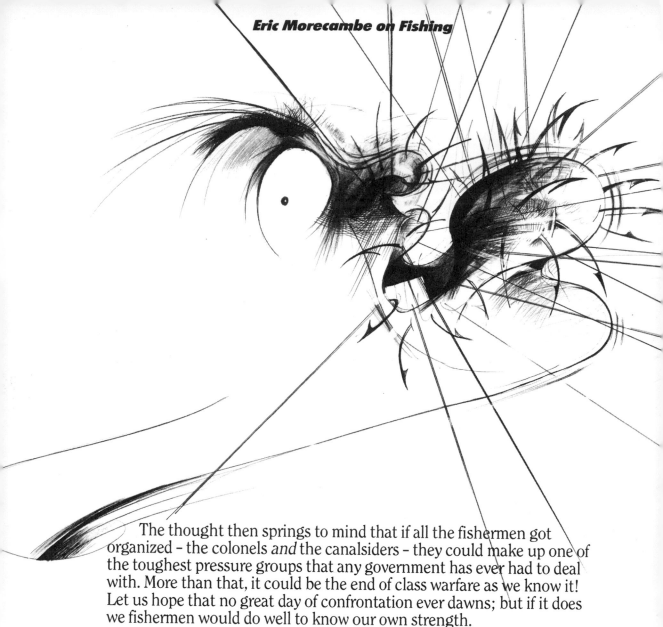

The thought then springs to mind that if all the fishermen got organized - the colonels *and* the canalsiders - they could make up one of the toughest pressure groups that any government has ever had to deal with. More than that, it could be the end of class warfare as we know it! Let us hope that no great day of confrontation ever dawns; but if it does we fishermen would do well to know our own strength.

WHEREVER NEXT?

Although we have our seasons for coarse and game fishing, no-one has told the fish. As a result, they will accept our baits, lures and flies just about all the year round. The seasons are part of a system of man-made rules, and we stick to them because it makes sense to respect the breeding patterns of the fish and not to overwork the waters they live in. Nevertheless, you can find variations.

Trout fishing on the River Test is from May to September, but on the local reservoirs near my home they start around the beginning of March. Finding a place to fish is really a bit like getting a drink in a pub or hotel. If you try hard enough, and are prepared to travel around a bit – like to the old Covent Garden market in the early hours of the morning – you can always get one. With trout, too, there's always somewhere open.

You may have to go abroad, but that is usually no hardship. Not to me, it isn't, although I must say I haven't yet been abroad on an out-and-out fishing holiday. Blame it on the wife, if you like, but on a family holiday we always prefer to go around together and do the same things. Joan isn't interested in fishing, and my son prefers coarse fishing, so we aren't exactly three minds with but a single thought. Blame it on work as well. I have had one or two nice offers of trips abroad but couldn't go because I had to work for some or all of the period of the holiday.

Before the 1982 World Cup, I was invited to go to Spain and do a commentary for New Zealand Radio on the New Zealand team. That would give me two weeks in Spain – they didn't expect the team to last more than three games – and then we hit the real perk. This was to fly, with my wife, to New Zealand for six weeks of trout fishing in the big lakes they have there. I couldn't do it, for the simple reason that I was working. It's funny, that, but it always seems to happen. On the other hand, I've had plenty of times when I've wanted to work and couldn't get a job. There's no justice . . .

The really big trips for the holiday fisherman take him nowadays to places like Iceland and Alaska. Just the sort of country you've always wanted to visit? Probably not – if you aren't a fisherman. If you are, and money is little or no object, then a magnificent holiday awaits.

I have several friends whose addiction for hanging about near the

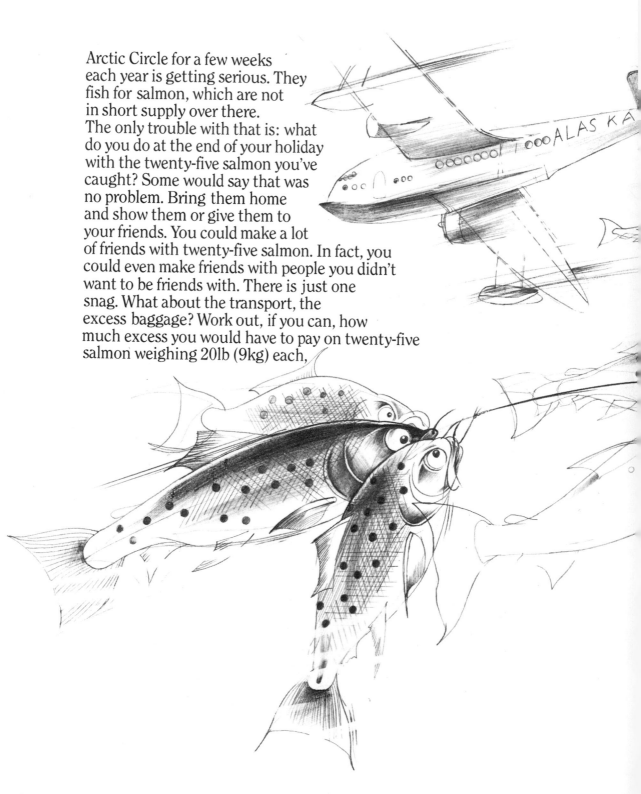

Arctic Circle for a few weeks
each year is getting serious. They
fish for salmon, which are not
in short supply over there.
The only trouble with that is: what
do you do at the end of your holiday
with the twenty-five salmon you've
caught? Some would say that was
no problem. Bring them home
and show them or give them to
your friends. You could make a lot
of friends with twenty-five salmon. In fact, you
could even make friends with people you didn't
want to be friends with. There is just one
snag. What about the transport, the
excess baggage? Work out, if you can, how
much excess you would have to pay on twenty-five
salmon weighing 20lb (9kg) each,

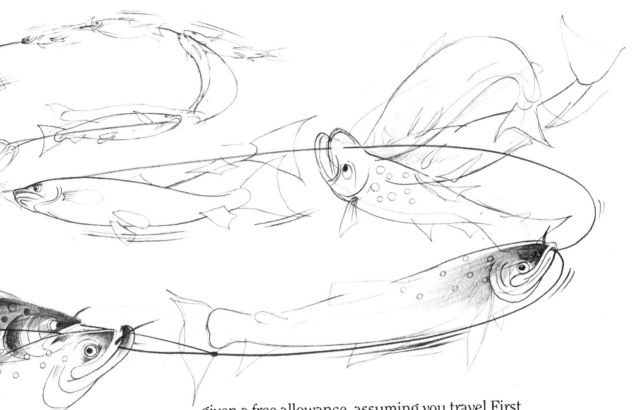

given a free allowance, assuming you travel First
Class (which you would) of 66lb (30kg) with unlimited excess (which
you wouldn't get) charged at a rate to be agreed with the airline.

Not easy. The upshot is, my friends come home with about four fish
each, which they have had smoked to get their weight down as far as
possible.

Now, they will forgive me, but I don't altogether see the point of
that. It may sound a bit eccentric but if I had caught twenty-five salmon
in Alaska, I'd want to bring the whole lot home. It may not be easy, but
that is what I would want to do. When I got them back here, I wouldn't
necessarily give them away, not all of them; I expect I would invest in an
enormous freezer and stick them in there while I thought about it for a
few weeks. After all, if I could afford a medium-sized fortune to go and
catch fish in Alaska, I could certainly afford an enormous freezer to
house them in back home. Any offers?

ON
SEA
FISHING

I haven't a lot to say about sea fishing, for the simple reason that I don't do it. I have done it, as I mentioned earlier, out in the middle of Morecambe Bay in my extreme youth. I was, by the way, a very extreme youth, and sometimes caught more than the rest of our boat put together, which made me fairly unpopular as a twelve- or thirteen-year-old sat amongst the Dads. But all that is in the past. Sea fishing is no longer for me. Not after Torquay.

I was playing a summer season at one of the theatres in the 'Queen of Watering Places.' My nephew, then aged twelve, came down to stay, and someone I had become quite friendly with invited us to go out mackerel fishing in his boat. I thought it would be an experience for the nephew, and anyway I fancied going myself.

Next day we chugged out across the flattest sea you could have wished for. Our host and captain selected a spot to fish from, then cut the engine and anchored. We started throwing out the feathers, which work on the same principle as spinners, and settled down to fish for a while. Gently the water slapped against the side of the boat. The sun shone through a slight haze of cloud.

We had made an early start and soon it was time for some breakfast. We ate a hearty breakfast that day. I saw mine twice. Once when I ate it, and again afterwards. The sea was still like a millpond; you could not see any waves. But there was this fatal slight motion which went slap . . . slap . . . slap on the side of the boat. That was the giveaway, and the cause of our undoing.

Our host and captain was all right, but my nephew and I were profusely sick. I am even prepared to swear that I have never felt so ill in my life, and my nephew was green. Before that day I had never quite understood the expression 'So-and-so turned green.' Then I saw my nephew and he was GREEN. I suppose I was too, but never got round to asking for a mirror.

Our host and captain could not understand it. He thought he had invited a keen fisherman and his nephew out for a morning's sport. I

could tell he was having some difficulty coping with the situation because he kept offering us more things to eat and drink.

'Would you like a coffee?'

'Err. No thank you.'

'Are you sure you wouldn't like a coffee, Mr Morecambe?'

Very softly: 'Yes.'

'Something stronger?'

Even more softly, and staring with glazed eyes out to sea: 'No . . . thank . . . you.'

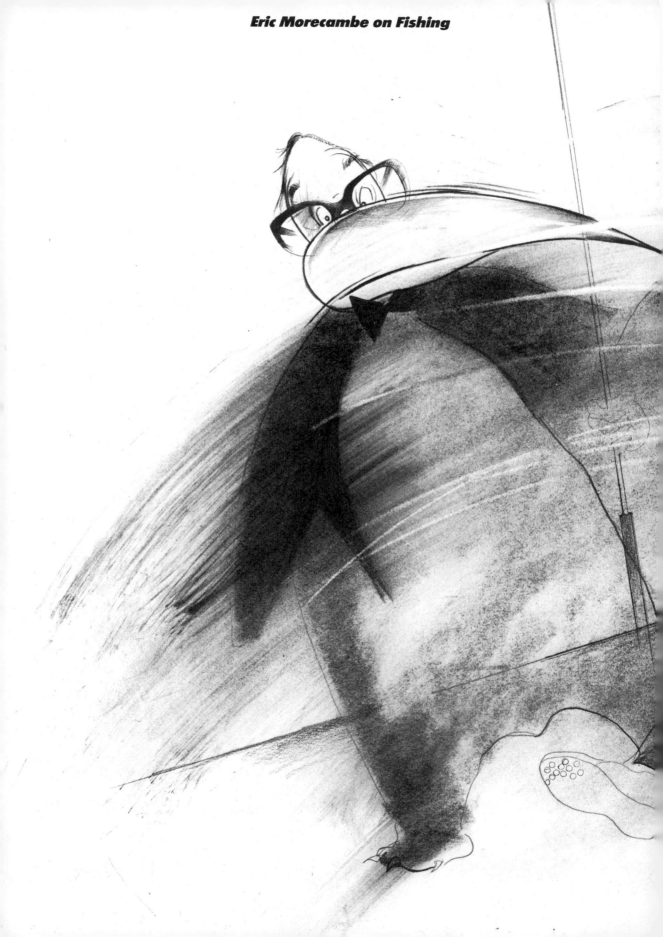

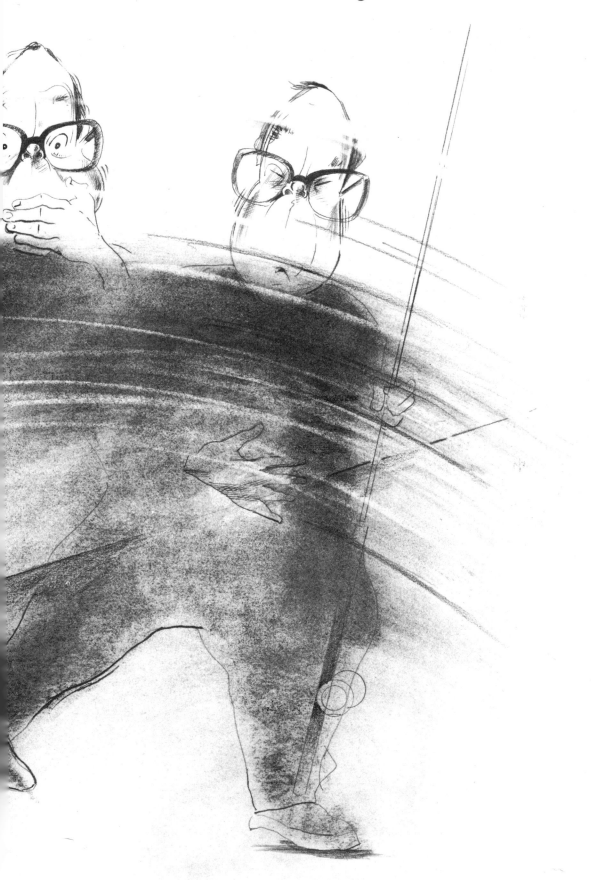

'I've got a stout here. If you'd like one?'

The words will not form any more. The mouth is open. Breathing is heavy. Sweat begins to stand out in beads on the forehead. The waves go slap . . . slap . . . slap . . . on the side of the boat . . . on the side of the . . .

'Yaaaeerghhh!'

In between these unfortunate breaks we actually caught fish. In fact we didn't feel so bad when we were occupied with the business of getting in the mackerel. We were all right, too, while the engine was running. But when it stopped, and we sat alone on the millpond rocking ever so gently from side to side . . .

Yes, well, we've gone into that already. All I will add is that, when we came ashore after our two hours on the English Channel, I was conscious of two things. The first was that I had a show to do that night; the second was that the world was still going from left to right, then right to left. I was weaving about the quayside like a distressed penguin.

How those people manage to sail round the world in a bathtub, wearing a top hat and filming the whole epic for simultaneous transmission on television, I shall never know, and I have no intention of trying to find out. Since that morning in Torquay I have never been back to sea in a small boat. Nor has my nephew, who was visibly aged by the experience. In fact he is now eighty-three and living below ground in a renovated Anderson shelter near Northampton; further from the sea he could not get.